:cking St Acklist St Acklet St Acte St Actometer St Ad St Adda St Addle St Addling St Ade St Adholder St A
dholdership St Adia St Adial St Atic St Adie St Adiomete St Adionicest St Adium St Adthaus St Adtho
Affed St Affer St Affette St Afful St Affier St Affish St [barcode] P9-DTN-364 Affords
g St Agarth St Agbeetle St Age St Ageable St Agean St A [barcode] St Ag ggerer
t Ager St Agerite St Agery St Agese St Agey St Aggard St [checkmark] P9-DTN-364 ggerer
ggers St Aggery St Aggon St Aggy St Aghe St Aghead St Aghcaded St Agnorn St Agnound St Agiary St A
n St Agirite St Agiritic St Agma St Agmoid St Agnal St Agnance St Agnancy St Agnant St Agnate St Agn
gnation St Agnatory St Agnature St Agne St Agnes St Agnicolous St Agnize St Agnum St Agon St Agy St A
Ahlism St Aid St Aidlin St Aidly St Aidness St Aie St Aig St Aighe St Aik St Aile St Aill St Ain St Ain
ll St Aincher St Aine St Ained St Ainer St Ainful St Aining St Ainless St Ainy St Ainyell St Air St Aircase S
ead St Airless St Airway St Airy St Ait St Aithe St Aithman St Aitly St Aive St Ack St Ake St Aked St A
ter St Al St Alactic St Alactical St Alactiform St Alactital St Alactite St Alactited St Alactites St Alactitic St .
ctitious St Alagma St Alagmite St Alagmitic St Alagmitical St Alagmometer St Alan St Alboat St Alch St
led St Alely St Alemate St Aleness St Alenge St Alewarde St Aling St Alk St Alkable St Alked St Alker St
St Alklet St Alko St Alky St All St Allage St Alland St Allange St Allar St Allary St Allatio St Allboat St
er St Aller St Allfed St Allfeed St Alling St Allingken St Allion St Allionize St Allite St Allnet St Allon St A
n St Alp St Althe St Altic St Alume St Alwarth St Alwartism St Alwartize St Alwartly St Alwartness St Alw
St Alworthness St Alworthy St Am St Amber St Ambook St Ambouline St Ambuck St Amele St Amen St A
Amina St Aminal St Aminate St Amineal St Amineous St Aminidium St Aminiferous St Aminigerous St A
St Aminose St Aminous St Ammel St Ammer St Ammerer St Ammering St Ammet St Amnose St Amp
ndgo St Ampant St Amped St Ampede St Ampee St Amper St Ampian St Ampine St Amping St Ampom
Ance St Anch St Anchel St Ancher St Anchgrain St Anchier St Anching St Anchion St Anchioned St Anch
St Andardbearer St Andardism St Andardization St Andardized St Andardizer St Andardwing St Andardwi
St Andelwelks St Andelwort St Andenguss St Ander St Andergrass St Andfast St Andfra St Andful St And
Andingstone St Andish St Andle St Andoff St Andout St Andpat St Andpipe St Andpoint St Andsill St Ar
Anerie St Anery St Ang St Angster St Anhope St Anhoscope St Aniel St Anitza St Ank St Anmarch St An
l St Anners St Annery St Annic St Annicle St Annide St Annier St Anniferous St Annified St Annine St A
o St Annotype St Annous St Annum St Anpicche St Ansel St Anssour St Anstickle St Ant St Antient St A
Ap St Ape St Apedectomy St Apedial St Apediform St Apedius St Apelia St Apes St Aphisacre St Aphisa
e St Aphyle St Aphyline St Aphylinid St Aphylococcus St Aphylolysin St Aphyloma St Aphyloplasty St Ap
phylotomy St Aphylotoxin St Aple St Apled St Aplefish St Apler St Appe St Apte St Ar St Aragen St Araj
lins St Arbright St Arch St Archamber St Arched St Archer St Arching St Archly St Archness St Archy St A
Areblind St Aree St Arer St Arf St Arfish St Arflower St Arful St Argaze St Argazer St Argazing St Argrass
St Aringly St Ark St Arkblind St Arkdead St Arken St Arkle St Arkled St Arkly St Arknaked St Arknaught S
ess St Arlet St Arlight St Arlighted St Arlike St Arling St Arlit St Arlitten St Arnel St Arnie St Arosta St Ar
r St Arrify St Arrily St Arriness St Arring St Arrulet St Arry St Arshine St Arshot St Arspangled St Arstone
St Arthistle St Arting St Artinghole St Artish St Artle St Artled St Artler St Artless St Artling St Artlish St A
up St Arty St Arvation St Arve St Arved St Arveling St Arven St Arver St Arving St Arvy St Arword St Arw
simetric St Asimon St Asimorphy St Asis St Assfurtite St At St Atable St Atal St Atant St Atarian St Atary
d St Atedly St Ateful St Atehood St Atehouse St Ateless St Atelet St Atelich St Atelihood St Atelike St At
nt St Atemonger St Ater St Atera St Ateroom St Atery St Atesman St Atesmancraft St Atesmanlike St Ate
nan St Athe St Athel St Athelfast St Athelness St Athely St Athmograph St Atical St Atically St Atice St A
t Ationar St Ationarily St Ationariness St Ationarity St Ationary St Ationed St Ationer St Ationery St Ation
Ationize St Ationmaster St Atiscope St Atism St Atist St Atistic St Atistical St Atistically St Atistician St At
Ative St Atization St Atize St Atizer St Ato St Ator St Atory St Atua St Atual St Atuarism St Atuarist St At
Atuesque St Atuette St Atuist St Atuized St Atuminate St Atuomania St Atuquoism St Atural St Ature St At
e St Atutably St Atuary St Atute St Atutebook St Atutemerchant St Atutestaple St Atutorily St Atutory St .
olism St Aulande St Aule St Aull St Aum St Aumrel St Aunch St Auncheon St Aunge St Aup St Aupings
St Aurolite St Aurolith St Auroscope St Aurotied St Aurotidiferous St Aurus St Aval St Ave St Aved St Ave
St Avy St Aw St Awbote St Awe St Awk St Awle St Awnche St Awyll St Axis St Ay St Ayathome St Ayed S
St Ayle St Ayless St Aysail St Ayship St Aytape St Chi St Ead St Eadable St Eade St Eadfast St Eadfasthead S
fastship St Eadful St Eady St Eadier St Eadily St Eadiment St Eadiness St Eading St Eadless St Eadship St E
Eakraid St Eal St Ealable St Ealage St Ealed St Ealer St Ealing St Ealf St Ealful St Ealfulness St Ealthily St
engine St Eamer St Eamily St Eaming St Eamroller St Eamship St Eamvessel St Eamwhistle St Eamy St
psin St Ear St Earate St Earerin St Earic St Earidge St Eariform St Earin St Earinery St Earing St Earne St
ne St Earyl St Easchist St Eath St Eatite St Eatitous St Eatization St Eato St Eatoid St Eatoma St Eatoma
osis St Eave St Eboy St Eccado St Ech St Echados St Echiometry St Eck St Eckle St Ed St Eddie St Edill St
Eeded St Eedless St Eek St Eeking St Eekkan St Eel St Eelback St Eelbow St Eelboy St Eeled St Eelen St E
ead St Eelheaded St Eelhearted St Eelhemp St Eelification St Eelify St Eeliness St Eeling St Eelle St Eel
te St Eelspring St Eely St Eelyard St Eem St Een St Eenbok St Eenbrass St Eene St Eening St Eenkirk St .
n St Eeper St Eepful St Eepiness St Eeping St Eepish St Eeple St Eeplechase St Eeplechaser St Eepled St Ee
St Eeplet St Eeplewise St Eeplish St Eeply St Eepness St Eepto St Eepup St Eepwise St Eepy St Eer St Eer
r St Eering St Eerish St Eerless St Eerling St Eerman St Eermost St Eersman St Eersmate St Eerswoman St E
Eever St Ef St Effne St Efhede St Eg St Eganography St Eganopod St Egh St Egnotic St Ego St Egoid St
St Eille St Eimming St Eimy St Ein St Einbock St Einbok St Einch St Eincheck St Eine St Einerian St Eing
Einmannite St Einzie St Eip St Eipell St Eire St Eirne St Eiryr St Eke St Ekelyng St Ela St Elar St Ele St El
liteutic St Ell St Ella St Ellaceous St Ellar St Ellaria St Ellary St Ellascope St Ellate St Ellated St Ellation St
e St Elled St Elleer St Ellie St Ellenbosch St Ellerid St Ellerine St Ellettide St Elleto St Ellifer St Elliferal S
ation St Ellified St Elliform St Ellify St Elligerate St Elling St Ellio St Ellion St Ellionate St Elliscript St Ell
y St Elth St Em St Emapod St Eming St Emless St Emlet St Emlings St Emma St Emmatiform St Em

Epull St Epup St Er St Eracle St Eradian St Erage St Erap St Erc St Ercobiln St Ercoraceous St Ercoraemia St Ercora
anist St Ercoranite St Ercorarian St Ercorarious St Ercorary St Ercorate St Ercoration St Ercorean St Ercoreous St Erc
Ercorist St Ercorolith St Ercorose St Ercorous St Ercory St Ercovorous St Erculia St Erd St Ere St Eregon St Erelmin
ma St Ereo St Ereobate St Ereochemistry St Ereochrome St Ereochromy St Ereogram St Ereograph St Ereographic St E
hically St Ereography St Ereohome St Ereometer St Ereometrian St Ereometric St Ereometrical St Ereometry St Ereon
Ereoscope St Ereoscopic St Ereoscopically St Ereoscopism St Ereoscopist St Ereoscopy St Ereotomy St Ereotype St
er St Ereotypic St Ereotyping St Ereotypist St Ereotypographer St Ereotypy St Erep St Ereynge St Erhydraulic St Eri S
St Erigma St Eril St Erile St Erilifidianism St Erility St Erilizable St Erilization St Erilizator St Erilize St Erilizer St E
rlet St Erling St Erlinge St Erlingly St Erlingness St Erlit St Ern St Erna St Ernad St Ernage St Ernal St Ernalgia S
d St Ernchase St Ernebra St Erned St Erner St Ernet St Ernfast St Ernful St Ernhead St Erniform St Ernine St Ernite St
an St Ernmost St Ernness St Erno St Ernon St Ernpost St Ernsheet St Ernshoots St Ernsman St Ernson St Ernum St E
St Ernutative St Ernutatory St Ernward St Ernwheel St Erny St Erope St Erquilinian St Erquilinious St Erracle St Err
Errep St Errile St Errometal St Errop St Erte St Ertel St Ertor St Ertorious St Ertorous St Ertylle St Eryn St Et St Ete S
gram St Ethograph St Ethometer St Ethophone St Ethoscope St Ethy St Etprocessus St Euard St Euch St Eudiant St Eve
Even St Evened St Evenet St Evin St Ew St Ewable St Eward St Ewardess St Ewardly St Ewardry St Ewardship St Ewa
St Ewat St Ewdiant St Ewed St Ewfe St Ewhouse St Ewin St Ewing St Ewish St Ewpan St Ewpot St Ewth St Ewy St
Byer St Eyl St Eylling St Eyme St Eynch St Eyn St Eyp St Eyre St Eyvyne St Foin St Henia St Henic St I St Iarne St I
bial St Ibialism St Ibiarian St Ibiate St Ibiated St Ibic St Ibiconite St Ibie St Ibilite St Ibine St Ibio St Ibious St Ibium St
Ibogram St Iborn St Ica St Icados St Iccado St Icche St Ich St Iche St Ichados St Ichering St Ichewort St Ichic St Ichi
Ichochrome St Ichoi St Ichology St Ichomancy St Ichometric St Ichometrical St Ichometry St Ichomythia St Ichomy
chwort St Ick St Ickage St Icke St Icked St Icker St Ickfree St Ickful St Ickin St Ickiness St Icking St Ickingpiece St Ick
er St Ickingpoint St Ickinthemud St Ickish St Ickit St Icklac St Ickle St Ickleback St Ickler St Ickling St Ickout St Ickpe
ictic St Id St Iddy St Idfastliche St Idie St Idy St Ie St Iebkin St Ied St Iel St Iele St Iep St Ier St Ieridge St Ierne St Iew
Iffenbodied St Iffener St Iffening St Iffing St Iffish St Iffler St Iffly St Iffneck St Iffner St Iffness St Ifle St Ifleburn St
Ifner St Ift St Ig St Ight St Ightle St Ightler St Ightly St Igian St Igma St Igmal St Igmaria St Igmat St Igmatal St Igma
al St Igmatiferous St Igmatiform St Igmatism St Igmatist St Igmatization St Igmatize St Igmatized St Igmatizing St Ig
St Igmatypy St Igme St Ih St Ik St Ike St Ikelunge St Ilbene St Ilbid St Ilbite St Ildegrain St Ile St Iletta St Ilette St I
Ilking St Ill St Illado St Illage St Illant St Illatim St Illation St Illatitious St Illatory St Illbirth St Illborn St Illburnt St I
St Illeli St Illen St Iller St Illery St Illet St Illgreen St Illhead St Illhouse St Illhunt St Illhunter St Illhunting St Illiard
Illicide St Illicidious St Illicidium St Illie St Illified St Illiform St Illing St Illian St Illish St Illitorie St Illlife St Illness S
Illsitting St Illstand St Illwater St Illworth St Illy St Illyard St Ilonovo St Ilp St Ilpnomelane St Ilpnosiderite St Ilt S
Iltified St Iltiness St Ilting St Iltish St Ilton St Ilty St Ilus St Im St Ime St Imie St Immer St Impart St Imulable St Imula
ant St Imulate St Imulating St Imulation St Imulative St Imulator St Imulatory St Imulatress St Imulatrix St Imule St In
St Inch St Inck St Ine St Ing St Ingeree St Inged St Inger St Inghum St Ingily St Inginess St Inging St Ingle St Ingless S
St Ink St Inkard St Inkardly St Inker St Inkhorn St Inkibus St Inking St Inkingly St Inkingness St Inkpot St Inkston
d St Int St Intage St Intance St Intch St Inted St Inter St Intily St Inting St Intless St Inty St Iony St Ip St Ipate St Ipatie
St Ipella St Ipellate St Ipend St Ipendary St Ipended St Ipendial St Ipendiarian St Ipendiarist St Ipendiary St Ipendiate
ess St Iper St Ipes St Ipiform St Ipit St Ipitate St Ipites St Ipitiform St Iple St Ipone St Ipound St Ipple St Ippled St Ipp
st Ippyant St Iptic St Ipula St Ipulaceous St Ipulane St Ipulant St Ipular St Ipulary St Ipulate St Ipulated St Ipulation St
Ipule St Ipulean St Ipuled St Ipuliferous St Ipuliform St Ipulode St Ipulose St Ipye St Ir St Irabout St Irage St Irdy St Ir
St Iria St Iriate St Iricide St Irious St Irk St Irket St Irless St Irling St Irment St Irom St Irometry St Irop St Irp St Iripicu
Irrage St Irrah St Irrance St Irrand St Irre St Irred St Irree St Irrer St Irring St Irringly St Irrup St Irrupcup St Irrupiron
ess St Irrupoil St Irup St Itch St Itchback St Itched St Itchel St Itchen St Itcher St Itchery St Itching St Itchmeal St Itchwo
St Ithil St Ithly St Ithly St Itic St Itlebagge St Itling St Ittleback St Ittystitty St Ive St Iver St Ivour St Ivy St Iward St Iv
h St Oage St Oak St Oat St Oater St Oave St Ob St Obball St Obber St Obe St Oberlie St Obhert St Obill St Oburne St
do St Ocah St Ocbred St Occade St Occado St Oce St Ochastic St Ochiometry St Ock St Ockade St Ockaded St Ocka
t St Ockard St Ockbridge St Ockbroker St Ockcard St Ockdove St Ocked St Ockenapple St Ocker St Ockexchange St O
gillyflower St Ockholder St Ockily St Ockinet St Ocking St Ockingapple St Ockinged St Ockinger St Ockingett St Oc
ne St Ockingless St Ockintrade St Ockish St Ockjob St Ockjobber St Ockjobbying St Ockkeeper St Ockless St Ocklo
rket St Ockoftrade St Ockstill St Ocktaker St Ocktaking St Ockwork St Ocky St Ocyen St Oddy St Ode St Odge St Od
Odul St Ody St Oechados St Oechas St Oechiogeny St Oel St Oep St Of St Offado St Ofne St Og St Oggie St Ogy
St Oically St Oicheiology St Oicheiomatical St Oicheiometry St Oicheiotical St Oician St Oicism St Oicity St Oicize S
St Oir St Oisen St Oit St Oiter St Ok St Okagag St Oke St Okehold St Okehole St Oker St Okerage St Okerless St O
St Okyn St Okyng St Ol St Ola St Olated St Olch St Olde St Oldred St Ole St Oled St Olen St Olethery St Olid St Oli
Olled St Oln St Olo St Olon St Oloniferous St Olp St Oltherie St Olyn St Olzite St Oma St Omacace St Omacal St Oma
achal St Omachate St Omached St Omacher St Omachful St Omachic St Omachical St Omaching St Omachious St On
y St Omachous St Omachy St Omager St Omapod St Omata St Omamatal St Omate St Omatic St Omatiferous St Oma
odaeum St Omatode St Omatopod St Omatous St Omber St Omble St Omere St Omele St Ommok St Omochor
aeum St Omok St Omp St Ompe St Omper St Ompneus St On St Onage St Onch St Ond St Onde St Ondard St Ondene
e St Oneage St Oneax St Oneblind St Oneblue St Oneboat St Onebow St Onebreak St Onebrod St Onebuck St Onec
at St Onecoal St Onecrop St Onecutter St Oned St Onedemel St Onedike St Onefly St Onefruit St Onegall St Onege St
St Onehore St Onehorse St Onejug St Onelath St Oneless St Onelet St Onelily St Oneman St Onemason St Onen
ne St Onepitch St Oner St Oneraw St Onern St Onery St Onesfield St Oneshot St Onesmatch St Onesthrow St Onest
all St Oneware St Oneweight St Onework St Onewort St Oney St Ong St Onge St Ongke St Onied St Onify St Onily St
sh St Onk St Onkerd St Onnard St Onne St Onnore St Ont St Onte St Ony St Onyhearted St Oo St Oobber St Ook St O
St Ookless St Ool St Oole St Oolen St Ooling St Oolle St Oolwork St Ooly St Oom St Oon St Oop St Oopandroop St O
allant St Ooping St Oor St Oot St Ooter St Ooth St Oothe St Oove St Oowre St Op St Opcock St Ope St Opel St Opell S
St Opine St Oping St Ople St Opless St Oppability St Oppage St Oppall St Opance St Oppe St Opped St Oppel St Op
ing St Opping St Opple St Oppull St Opsel St Opull St Opwatch St Opylle St Or St Orable St Oracke St Orage St Or
St Ordy St Ore St Ored St Oreful St Oreholder St Orekeeper St Oreman St Orer St Oreroom St Oreship St Oresman S

"What I have written has no plan, or at least is not planned. If it has a shape it is chiefly that it returns to its beginning. It has themes and a theme even if it wanders far. If it has a unity it is that what goes before conditions what comes after and *vice versa.*"

from *The Anathemata* by David Jones

"If we don't garden the tongue,
they'll blacktop it over."

Gerry Gilbert, in a letter

"And the Spirit of the Lord shall rest upon him, the spirit of wisdom and understanding, the spirit of counsel and might, the spirit of knowledge and the fear of the Lord."

Isaiah 11:2

"... And the number of gifts of the Holy Ghost is seven."

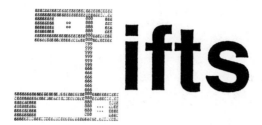

iven

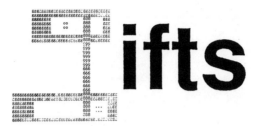

The Martyrology Book(s) 7 &

consisting of
ASSUMPTIONS (A Counting Bk VII—1984 to 1988)
ST. ANZAS: basis/bases (The Martyrology Bk (10)$_8$—1985 to 1988)
MONOTONES (1967 to 1972)
SCRAPTURES (1965 to 1972) etc. et al

```
b   p     n   i   c   h   o   l
a   l     e       a   o   l   a
s   u     i   n   n   l   d   n
s   n     t   o       d       g
    k     h   r       d       u
n   i     e   t       y       a
o   t     r   h       e       g
t         t   e       f       e
e         h           i
          e           n       r
              t       i       e
              h       t       a
              e       i       r
                      o       r
                      n       a
                      s       n
                              g
                      c       e
                      h       s
                      a
                      n       a
                      g       l
                      e       l

                      a
                      s       t
                              h
                              e
```

nouns and names   you

Coach House Press · Toronto

Quotations on the back cover are from bpNichol's "Narrative in Language: The Long Poem," first published in *The Dinosaur Review,* then reprinted in *Tracing the Paths,* edited by Roy Miki (Vancouver: Talonbooks, 1988).

Thanks to Nicky Drumbolis, Lola Tostevin and Ellie Nichol.—I.N.

Published with the assistance of the Canada Council and the Ontario Arts Council

Nichol, B. P., 1944–1988
    Gifts: the martyrology book(s) 7 &

Poems.
ISBN 0-88910-393-3

I. Title. II. Title: The martyrology book(s) 7 &.

PS8527.I32S53 1990   C811'.54   C90-095282-2
PR9199.3.N48G53 1990
        69565

To go beyond THE WORD.
exercise control over it? no
*NO **NO** — BEYOND THE*
WORD. not to merely control
it but to overcome it, go be-
yond the point where it is
even necessary to think in
terms of it

> Journal note
> Vancouver
> April 7, 1964
> 2:15 a.m.

for ellie
outside these books
that life

Middle Initial Event

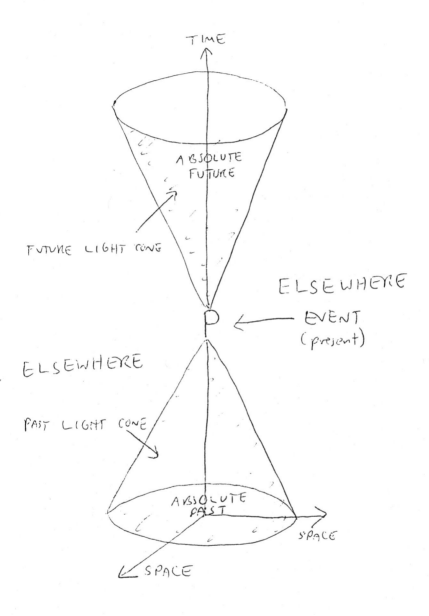

TIME

ABSOLUTE
FUTURE

FUTURE LIGHT CONE

ELSEWHERE

ELSEWHERE

EVENT
(present)

PAST LIGHT CONE

ABSOLUTE
PAST

SPACE

SPACE

June 12, 1988
(after diagrams by Stephen Hawking)

read, dear
For Birk Sproxton & Dennis Johnson

• july 2nd

at Sylvan Lake
sun going down
old hotel behind me
not a memory of
but the recollection
my parents dancing here
1933
their honeymoon
Uncle Earl playing in the orchestra
what song? what tune? what music
drifts across the water
all water
years
the self-conscious act of
memory
re-membering
a life, love, the i is born out of
passion
songs play
are replayed
the dance goes
on goes
on
        fam-ily
        fami-ly
        fam-ily
        fami-ly
        fam-i-ly
            -i-ly
            -i-
            -i-

• july 3rd

under the gray stairs
beside the white grocery store
the body of the cat
stiff now
death having taken it
where? looking round
up & down oliver road
tears streaming down my cheeks
1954
heaven?

• july 4th

notes
struck over & over again

chords
that stack up
play on something in you

resemblances/rhythms

rhymes
it takes a life time to hear

heard

• july 4th

this   blue   that

vocabulary

word choice or obsession
i.e. no choice at all
driven   &/or   dictated

this: present & therefore to be accounted for.
blue: all around you (sky   sea   the robin's egg you found aged 3).
that: other   past present future.

assumptions masking as givens
the way belief sits outside the rational

the way the senses ration the world
let only so much in

so much let in

letting

irrational

• july 4th

hi story
hi world
hi bee
      leaf

hell o honey
is the stinger
in the vision of
paradise
sin tax
of a life

a is for apple
b is for ball

it all comes down

it all comes down to

this

• july 5th (song)

moonin' around
coz i ain't with my honey

blue
coz i isn't with you

cat's got my tongue
makes me talk funny

when heaven ain't happenin'
hell has to do

• july 5th (rewriting an old poem from memory)

1934
my sister donna
died at my mother's breast
three months old

1955
i found her shoes in a box
no bigger than
my palm

• july 5th

things remembered or recalled

the way that old song refuses to leave the mind

alone

conversations with gone friends
how it seemed you would all go on
foreverie

/frag/mented/memory of /
beginnings   stories of
the world before you came to be

we are all
somebody's dead
baby

eventually

• july 6th

struck/sure

the search for absolutes
in a world of flux

where are we lead
when we follow their lead

what i read
is read, dear

only the pronunciation changes
not even moving your lips

pucker sucker

it's the kiss of life
of death

ellipsis

in which a little knowledge grows

and what's proposed?
a garden?
mind?

it ain't the thot changes, the spell's the same,
it's the attack rearranges the tone rows, the strings

          i signs
          i signifies
          i sings

• july 6th

tone not
tune nut

worm row
burrow or rub

mmmmm hmmmmm

mirror rim

!AHA!

• july 7th

reeding

get this mouth piece to work
adjust
        right?

clear a net
to catch the world in

string sections

rhythm

pi (an o's solution)

what it is, you say
words where the worlds dwell

use hey is what determines
meaning

hi
     (notes)
'lo
     (notes)
bi
     furcation

"it's my bag," pipes pal in drone
"you read the music so you can play"

"how still my heart

how high"

        the moon

• july 8th

at sylvan lake
certain things begin
or it is another
arbitrary point from which a line gets drawn
story has its start
its impulse
to unravel

the moon rises

a baby cries

outside the window
a cat prowls by &
an orchestra plays
"honey on the moon tonight"

sometimes
you think you see it all in the
mirror   rim
but then the light's dim or
your eyes fool you

the light's blue &
it's hard to read

the signs

flash on & off

"would you like to go dancing"

from memory

"take a chance & go romancing"

"i think i'd rather stay home &
read, dear."

Red Deer
1988

Scraptures: 7th Sequence

1

green yellow dog up. i have not. i am. green red cat down. i is not. i is.
over under upside up is. i's is not is i's.
           iffen ever never youd deside size seize says theodore
(green yellow glum) i'd marry you. truth heart hard confusions confess
all never neither tithe or whether with her lovers lever leaving her alone.
         no no.
                chest paws and chin.
                            no.

2

insect. incest. c'est in. infant. in fonts. onts. onts. ptonts. pontoons. la
lune. la lun.

la lun en juin est?
           c'est la lune from votre fenetre. vos. vouloir. i wish. i wish. i
may. i might. june night
    and the lovers
                  loafers, low firs, old frrrs, la lovers, la lrrrs.

3

liturgical turge dirge dinta krak kree fintab latlina santa danka schoen
fane sa paws claws le foret. my love coo lamna mandreen sont vallejo.
             oh valleys and hills lie open ingkra sintle
list la list cistern turning down.
         je ne sais pas madam. je ne sais pas mademoiselle.
je ne sais pas l'amour mirroring mes yeux meilleur my urging for you.

4

an infinite statement. a finite statement. a statement of infancy. a fine line
state line. a finger of stalemate. a feeling a saint meant ointment.

             tremble.
                a region religion
reigns in. a returning. turning return the lovers. the retrospect of
relationships always returning. the burning of the urge. the surge forward
in animal being inside us. the catatosis van del reeba rebus suburbs of our
imagination. last church of the lurching word worked weird in our heads.

5

great small lovers move home. red the church caught up relishes dog.
lovers sainthood loses oversur. oh i growing hopeless lies in ruin. u in i
hope beet root.

6

halo. hello. i cover red my sentiment. blankets return the running ships
back. clock. tock tock tick tock.
              so he loves her. the red dog green home. geth ponts returns a
meister shaft. statements each one and any you rather the could've
repent—alright? il n'est pas sont ecole la plume plum or apples in
imagining je ne desirez pause. je ne sais pas. je ne sais. je pas.

7

il y a la lever la lune. l'amour est le ridicule of a life sont partir dans
moors. le velschtang est huos le jardin d'amour, un chanson populaire in
the revolution.
                                        mon amour est un
cherie, a cherry, a cheery rose with shy petals to sly on. saint reat will
teach me songs to woo her.

8

au revoir. le reveille sounds up the coach. les pieds de la chevalier voleur
sont ma mere en la nuance de ma votoveto.
                    oh maman. oh papan pa pan pa pa pan pa
pan pan. le choux deriver la now du chien from dog. le chat cat is back
who has forgotten his name.

1967

•

ferry me across

all these journeys
all these bodies of water, air,
between this world
& some other
named or unnamed

all these readings of the current
waves   sines
            ⎧ embarkment
final dis ⎨
            ⎩ charge
on some other shore

all this striking of
cymbals/drumming/ringing
invisible bell
weather
wake of consciousness
how there can be only one true sign for God
H or El or
how the two together form a Hell
unspoken

because to speak the true name
presumes the power to invoke
not yours, outside the i
worlds we pass between

uncalm

prehending

Victoria to Vancouver
June 1, 1988
Assumptions

St. Anzas I

stanzas. stances.
st. anza me
please. definition's an equation
the liquidation of language
has nothing to do with
death
only flow
you are translated
among the wreckage
watch the ship grow
back together
in organic form
ill logic's heeled

mina d l abour
arbor or (within
—not a notion of—
but &) so
c

caffin so seeing
did & nothing
not even thant
repeat so repeat
sounds open did
ot
nor

the room's a metaphor
you walk thru
leaving bits of self
behind or symbolic
windows to open, storms up for winter
storms (as in the cab you didn't catch
up 5th avenue, faster to walk
finally) furnace on
shivering in the one a.m. transparency of your reflection

m n
d d d
doesn't this sound like
yes   & left this

connecting now   no
for a moment   r
l
  q
    f

g k s z
h v w a

too classical saints
conversing, almost, as if
heaven & the clouds parting
you walk up finally to your reward
which was earth, these breaks
in which your life takes
hold, is lived, incomplete or
again, the insistence,

nuh nuh
cal tume yah
r venter & r
oppose z oppose
really a pairing
peering, not that

suh suh
mmnn
all or most
(which is just)
not thant that
yet tea &

maybe the door opens
the room gains
coherence from these passages
entry in & out of
lives, histories, a narrative
indistinctions among the shadowed leavings
trees, people, furniture you refuse to open
finding too many messages there
what did the language say to you

verse

verse

nothing but the cat,
a strophe passes in & out of
focus, lens,
maybe the micro
chipped beginning of your imperfection
measured as is

kammin difkley
ends

n o t i
g o g
e
    z a i c
f
f

& more i had wanted
to say want to
of which this is a
begin sing: notes
(can you hear me); notes
(can they hear me); notes.

Monotones

all that summer   hot
driving back   up   past
the headwaters of
                        the humber
broken mills & dams
the country actual
the time confused
                        spring or
summer
            driving thru
into
        the hills of mono

mona

moaning a name from another time
not mine   no part of
my world

mona's hills   the miller's hills
hills the water came from
turned his wheels

                        his world

stone fences & bent boards piled up against the mind

my time &
my world
flowing over
                        into
the broken grass

"it is as if my grandfather's house were turning over with me.
where is the person that will save me?"

"it is only crying about myself
that comes to me in song."

XII

from fallingbrook the road turns down

turning round
sun stuck in my eye

        "don't you ever,
        you up in the sky,
        don't you ever get tired
        of having the clouds between you & us?"

& the moon rose
later that night
eclipsed by
        the earth's shadow

ten or twelve of us
watching from
        behind the barn

flames rose
into the dark sky

dancers shouting as
their shadows flowed out of them

XIII

terra

earth

mother of gods

who goes
before me?

thera
        the one
ra

& i follow

flow
      after

into the moon

Some Nets

for Paul Dutton

1

three days after (*) *the lightning hit it* / or the beat, (*) check this, i can play around it, with it, there / *what's left of* (*) *the barn* (*) *still smoulders in the sun* / unresolved (*) notes or chords, should've been of wood, (*) paper, burning / *sending clouds of smoke across* (*) *the highway* / dislocating / *darkness* / *son* / *i awoke into* / nets / *hearing the voices from the Fire Hall across the lake* (*) / i remember this, angry, i thot it was a party, felt foolish / *seeing the flickering lights above the trees* / start looking for ways out, of this diction / *knowing* (*) *something was happening* / is happening, not in the way you intended, the way (*) that's always intended, you don't intend that / *unable to* (*) *determine* (*) *till the next day* / that tone, as tho the unravelling of this one event made the whole complex that is the world make sense, that (*) misuse of metaphor / *it was the barn's burning had awakened me* / it was the barn (*) burning, not the world

(*) *and poetry is like this too* (*) / or can be, shouldn't be, contains those smug assurances that the whole thing is (*) containable / *voices that disturb your sleep* / "only great events can create a great literature" / *lines* (*) *you write down* / the daily life, what we call the "mundane" / *unable to determine till the next day* / or longer (*) even, centuries, millennia / *the true* (*) *nature of what has awakened you* / that longing, all these years, for this, freedom to be, simple / *or* (*) *those other lines* / the ones you meant to write, celebrating (*) the ordinary effort of being, shorn of the old idealization of heroism and suffering, an (*) imagination of (*) peace to inform those desires for it / *that smoulder within you* / desire to be written / *three days or more* / searching for (*) the tone / *and even tho you write them down* (*) / (*) the lines i mean, prayers / *there is a darkness there* / literal, as tho the words on the page were not the words inside your brain (*) the moment that you went to write them, no / *at the core* / some other phrase or sentence / *some source that is not yet tapped or* / not yet believed or / *fully listened to* / beyond the rhetoric of intent / *far below the visible surface* / right at the surface of this page / (*) *burning* (*) / these words are, worlds are, lives, (*) are

2

things remarked on, (yes) not remarked on, (no) connections / *the night the man drowned in the canal* / another, (yes) nameless body / *in front of our room on Reguliersgracht* / "ours," (no) transitory reference, (yes) Paul & me, using the room for sleeping mostly / *hand reaching up from the water* / (no) i didn't "see" it (no) / *not reaching us as we slept on, oblivious,* (yes) / the "news" was out there, what the newspapers thrive on, our bodies (yes) / *tho the crowds gathered,* (yes) *the police came,* / reporters, things you read about / *the boats dragged the water searching for him* / looking for signs on the surface (yes) / *we dreamt of nothing* (no) *or* / dreamt the fragments thru which our daily lives continue (yes) / *so many things we could recall none of them* (no) / intrusion of the discursive voice (yes) / *troubled all night by something we could not reach,* / could not understand / *someone calling to us,* (no) *or worse* / naming / *the absolute silence into which a plea for help can fall* (yes) (yes)

murmurings, indistinct voices &/or musics / *& the next day, the Hotelkeeper brought us breakfast,* / it was like that / *asked how we'd slept, we answered "fine,"* / a description / *not really thinking, assuming the usual exchange of vagaries,* / the empty words, the empty place, signs as signals of another order / *until he told us of the man who'd drowned* / just that / *underneath our window,* (yes) & put the breakfast tray down

3

at night, (at night) *looking out from the Lido* (at night) / hotel on the corner, (at night) river taxis tied to the docks below us (at night) / *the lights of Venice in the distance* (at night) / shining (at night) / *names,* (at night) *that they do invoke* (at night) / even a stranger's (at night) / & (at night) *in invoking* (at night) *evoke, call forth* / things that linger at the edge of perception / *into the bright sunlight sparkles off the water's choppy surface* / yes (at night)

being carried up the canal by water ferry (the next day) / retracing the route we had taken (the next day) / *past the stone fences in the fenced-in gardens* (the next day) / details of your life forgotten as rapidly as they occur (the next day) / *the decaying foundations & steps* (the next day) / flashbacks that lead nowhere (the next day) / *narrow landings into narrower courtyards* (the next day) / seeking for connections where none may exist (the next day) / *the boats plying their trade* (the next day) / working (the next day) / *gondoliers & all that quote romantic unquote garbage* (the next day) / thru & past you (the next day) / *adrift off the prow* (the next day) / detritus of thot forms (the next day) / *pressing towards Piazza le Roma* (the next day) / back sore from too much luggage (the next day) / *the train station beyond* (the next day) / not sure where we were going (the next day) / *naming* (the next day) / in a strange language (the next day) / *& on* (the next day) / yes (the next day)

Rice Lake/Amsterdam/Venice/Toronto
July 17, 1985, thru March 1988
Assumptions

t

he

in   in

be

g

NING

the

.   O   as

rew

th

er   gOd   ew

n

l

y

as

WHO IS
ALL THINGS

ndth

E

rew

    as

       aw

          or

             ds

          po

       ke

    ng

rew

an
yw
or
db
ei
ng

GOD'S

Diatribe

for Jim Smith

1

poly ticking of the world clock
running down
down at the heels
makes an ending of it all

you can't block out
blank out the world

out

damned spots before your eyes

heaviness
                of quotation
                of certain emotions

i'd love another glass of wine

                of that red
                of that read back to you

at the tone
the time

2

"a poetry claiming innocuously to be about language"*

what poetry's about

the language of war
the language of love
the language of presidents, prime ministers, premiers

this language of p's
more hopefully peace
middle initial me or you
public, polis, place

a language
of treaties
between peoples
treatises
treat us
as chattel, nouns, (worse)
never modifiers of their speech or
purpose

which is why i've become interested in very deliberately long and ugl
y lines
things that stick out or don't quite fit in
not a variable margin but the assumptions & how
we live everything at the margin or
marginally, return to
it

3

saint ratas   & his hierarchies

all that old information   puntification

only the technology changes
the deaths the same
the suffering

                        ugliness of this
                        this poem
                        thing

                                        part of my art

i fact
we fact too

hell
what's here the daily paper doesn't tell you?

only the words
their compressions

breaks

like a mind

adamizes

brings eve down

no one left to sing your praises mother

no language

earth

4

"to help the rearguard action of those of us who wish to subvert cur-
rent trends toward poetic-linguistic navel-gazing and solipsism."

this part of the poem
is for Kit James
who blew up a police station in California in the sixties
part of the Black Panther action
came north into Canada
his sense of things changing
eating all the left-over food
off the tables in the restaurant we sat in
telling me about that transparent door he looked thru
into another world or universe
spirit, being,
the last time i saw him
before he went north, further,
drowned in some northern lake
as i was informed by letter, later,
gone thru, a door
ation, translation, a poem for
the contradictions, the shifts between
actions, states, over the border
lines which do not lead you into the
of reason none the less
of language or
th'ought
what presses you on
the innocuousness of daily speech
the deaths it leads to
because we do not hear clear
ly see
where language is leading to

5

ecstasy of clear speaking

or that dialogue opens
     di mensions

and that when the one
speaks for the two
(or tries to)
for the tribe   hoped for or imagined
diatribe   all these voices scream as one thru you
shrilling above the babble towers over us

not prophetic then
simply the sheer weight of what language is
asserting itself against the misuse & abuse of tongues
assaults us daily
word killers
who work thru the cheapening of all the terms we hold most
dear
till there is no way, simply, to say

diatribe
lest the tribe die
i's wanting to be heard

Assumptions

---

* David Manicom in a review of Gary Geddes' *Twentieth-Century Poetry and Poetics* as published in *Rubicon* 6 (Montreal, 1986).

early morning variation

di
agon al
y

      die
al
   in agony

a gone y
a hip s
a ship

shhh

i is p
"under what conditions?"
unclear

uncle ear
auntie tongue

"i am against no one"

an e at noon
an s at night
the y gone
             shipped out to sea
d
  e f g
      h
i j k
l ephant
om
   e
equals mc^2
how to
find my way back from
these letters
         sounds you sent me
out into the world to find
found
     the world reduced to

its codes
        systems
the plants grow on
obsolescent images
art facts

without the i f acts

we fear f's ear
dead arms close round us
rigor mort is the one
removes our lungs
         seals our face
f's ace up the sleeve
ning
    variations
between the real & the reeled in
monsters from the seas we sail
(contra the old dogma of supremacy)

the unknown unfolds as
the known folds over & is undone

    STATEMENT: Of Ath: "C's land, eh Stein?"

        (translation:
        De Ath: "Stein? Est-ce que le terre du C?"

relationships to figures

1 &

s's cape a shroud
sweet sibilance piercing the tongue
lead by the one i did not recognize
deeper into language
the lung images
the mind
        simpler forms of speech
signs
      showing me this other world
the landscape lay behind

    1973

Scraptures: 4th Sequence

DREAM

(a dream

drama

)

AM RED

am green

am green

am groen

am green

AM GREEN

AM GREED

am greed
am greed

am greed
am greed

am greed
am greed

a   greed

a greed

agreed

agree

AGREE

ATREE

a tree
a treet

a treat
as treat

as treat
has treat

HA!!!!!!!

St. Reat

AH!!!!!!!!!!!!!!!!!!!!!!!!!!!!!!!!!!!!!!

DREAMDREAM D R E A M D R

ream r e a m ream r e

E A M E A

A W A K E

a w a k e awake a w a k e

AWAKEA W A K EA W A K E A W A

"I have forgotten you
St. Reat. I am sorry
St. Reat. I am not."

"St. Reat I was forgotten

by you. Are you sorry?
Are you really St. Reat
you know I'm not my St."

who was st. reat?
who was sorry?
who is st. reat?
who is sorry?
who shall st. reat be?
who shall be sorry?

¿forgotten?

St. Reat?

Generations

driving 7 north to 15 36 Plunkett from 80 Regina 4 Sarah & 6 25 Ellie in 72 50 1 the car beside me 3 auto 18 21 bi 2 ogra 40 phy 29 24 13 nothing to do with 9 me? 17 44 the car i'm 45 carried in 52 68 beside these lines 90 lead their 91 bro 5 ken 67 way 32 thru 99 35 85 Saskatchewan

Watrous 61 11 Manitou 33 Beach the 83 14 71 dance hall Ma was 8 courted in 19 by Pa 46 77 others 23 58 ac 59 cidental 39 couplings of 27 history 0 i.e. 56 circumstance 87 choices 31 53 82 made 10 givens ac 64 cepted 93 the 38 dance hall 54 55 closed now 12 when we pass 26 94 thru 62 lone 60 car on 92 28 89 this road this 95 hot May day

buffalo beans in 42 the 37 roadside 70 ditches 88 95 dandelions on 16 the 30 few ragged 22 lawns we drove on 74 75 into Plunkett 87 20 meadow larks 63 singing 86 98 in the heat 34 singed 43 fields 76 96 passed the old 48 hotel 66 mainly a 97 41 bar now 73 liquor 47 49 my grandfather would never have tolerated 78 stopped to 65 visit 79 Ma's cousin 57 no one home 69 51 left at 84 the Yellowhead 81 Route 16 100 west 137 into 122 Saskatoon

fever 113 dreams in this 126 127 heat 107 30o C & 131 rising 140 123 passing the 138 tiny graveyard where 102 my 101 great grandparents 135 109 lie 125 blue 132 sloughs 129 absolute of the prairie sky 105 139 caught up in 117 family 110 directions 124 designs 136 auto ma tic writing 103 134 nervous 111 system registering 118 the signals 121 128 counting 114 115 116 ones before our destination 104 106 108 119 ones 112 we'll never even see 120 133 130 we never even see

Saskatchewan/Toronto
May 1986/April 1988
Assumptions

Scraptures: 2nd Sequence

WAR

WARe

wHERE

whhhhhhhhhhhhhhhhhhhhhhhhhhhhhh

whhhhhhhhhhhhhhhhHHHHHHH

whhhhhhhhhhhhhhhhhhhhhhhhhhhhhhhh

air

Hair
Heir

air
eir **E**

HE

HarE

WarE

WE

bE

Ware

BE

ware

BEe

war

Be

wEar

weB

Ear

be

e

r

St. Anzas VIII

he he. stop that. just a joke
really. sssss. did you even think it thru
sir? pent-up emotion or
down mood. e-
quate them. quit then. no
's eye ears it this way. say?
same thing. s & then the a
prior i prior he. si.

junkyard let trembling, new
locales to cancer warlord presently. aldermen. grapes. "Or
whatever," she says, fingering butter son of a bitch dead languages.

rough somebody quick waiting, gone
profile mistaken.

sh. together
quietens the scream, anguish anyway. anxiety
lived with. terror. t's error &
s's in—in everything
really, st she say (the triple play
he's dealing with, bases loaded
try another way, base 5 or 10
(refigure the equation))

sitting sideways, hound or horse,
grief hugging blink daybed. ancient nicotine.
gravel all desktop hinder or
rambunctious. curled eyelid drip
vertical tinned.

so mulch for thatch.

she. sex talk. he. sf/x talk's
s's ex talk, gentle gender. what's out there? i's he. i she.
i dent i. fie yourself! we we we. all the way home.

Scraptures: 8th Sequence

NOW THIS IS THE DEATH OF POETRY. i have sat up all night to write you this—the poem is dying is dying—no—i have already said the poem is dead—dead beyond hope beyond recall—dead dead dead

granted a few quiet moments i would tell you what the poem is or has been since the poem is now dead. the poem has been nothing the poem has been something the poem is a has been has been ever this poem the same for me who would tell you now what it was to explain what it could be or might have been (as they say) MIGHT HAVE BEEN beyond recall now i have said but still having sat up all night i would tell you something of all this.

this is yours st. reat yours i know it is yours because it is not mine tho i write you now to tell you it is not mine (mine never having been ever and ever as always what has been said i said was said by you saint reat

so now i can tell you the breath is dead that brought forth the song (poem) long time gone old dear old poem yur a long time gone and i cannot do more now anything to bring you (him) (it) back no nothing no thing at all to bring the poem (song) back even tho i cry for it to say a part of me has a hunger that will not be eased (again & again) by speech (an old form) no for the form is dead that brought it forth

ACTUAL FACTUAL THE DEATH REPORTED TODAY TO ANY-ONE WHOLE WHO'LL LISTEN TO ME

as a friend would say it is over beginnings and endings say nothing not even middles used to i have confused you my people my people who are you listen to me who are you i do not know who i am today

maybe i will know now that the poem is dead

the poem imprisoned me (who he was) (i called him saint reat) imprisoned me till i could see no further into me beyond the poem that everything must be said in the poems form that the poem must say everything I HAVE NO TONGUE NO EYES i love with the poem SPEAK SPEAK and the language will not will you speak to me listen to me speak to me poem you will not would not you cannot hear me even you have become closed to me

as all poems must i have said i have said before as i have said many things before before now before i said what i said (to who? to saint reat against the forest fence fence of saint agnes a friend called her the same who saw saint reat and called saint agnes to him to her to he who waits to she who is now and forever trapped beyond the poem where saint reat lies dead (how he was born there of the eye and not the tongue) dead as i said against a fence where saint agnes saw him and a friend said he is dead and i knew it to be true.

•

lady of the assumption

mother muse

concept with which i am
uneasy
tho woman moved me
into the world
             not just a concept
conceived me
             carried me
house mother
             i was the nave
birthed from her arching body
– jack of hearts
– jack of all trades
– jack à cardiac
lord's drol
             wit has its play
ma i am
muse sum
o.k.? o
i know we share that common origin
your mother before you
her mother
             i went another way
male drop
        post card
which is why i say what i can
iconic
      coz the letter went as trey
double term   creates a third   dubs all terms
– tongue
– tongue
– tongue
there is a mouth you came from
can never return to
flap in this old skull until
your eyes turn inward and you're done

Assumptions

St. Anzas VI

three that end the same way
or did once, before revision hey?!
i saw the whole thing all over again
differently—the clouds, the gate—patterns,
rhythms   against which st.
anzas   or out of which the core
us looks for answers among the shifting
illusions
illuminations
illustrations any language allows.
alaws. rules by which the light flows thru
into this dim
ensions where the tongue's tension
                              be   holds it

or din
savage nary
crisp as in broken
ten latterly
none

simple as the
is is
flat & in the difference
dawn or any garden
just so if waiting apoplectic
pollenized

nothing's as simple as it seems,
as dense. the st. icks,
the st. ones, break the bones of
naming. the nouns
hurt you, hem you in
you look for clearings in the throat, to dance—
phlegmenco

diff rich
ridden roared
assumptive alliteration. quantum mince
leaden roads along above which
on the other overcast
flat latitudes among the glistening

seven to simple longings as attitudes
sordid dreaming
essential inference & then
lovely   lovely   lovely

flour essence. light from which the flower grows,
fills the head. ai of faith, slothfulness,
ah the daze
which is de a z of being,
or the slo thfulness ought to be shared,
to search for radical marks, question?
's definition, surely, nothing sure there
or sure is there
there for sure
there

clung

segmented

if of shift
of life

reasonable rack

dissent

light made lighter without the i

Scraptures: 16th Sequence
for david aylward

a tiny blue. a green. eastern and western. certain possible things. magic in the guise of science. shaman.

david sat down. plasmen. a door opened. outside the sky was blue and tiny. the grass was green. david sat down and talked. personal saints. words. we held up the sky. later i said blue. it was a tiny day. so little room to move in.

saint ranglehold. saint reat. saint agnes. saint and.

we moved into the room. a tiny green. a blue. hello. david opened a door. we talked of personal things. possible skys. saints. an eastern green. a western blue. tiny doors opening into the sky.

.

war.

raw.

and were i to give you   the moon. a clear sky. david said i was wrong.
opening the pages   *a million dollars.*

i felt like shit.

later it was all a lie.

.

the dream. saints appeared on the wall. ranglehold. reat. agnes. and. i was wrong. they were always there.

lunacy. phases of the moon. *a disturbing preoccupation.*

CHAPTER 36. david closed the book. blues for oleg. the circuit closed.
              (i want to let you in! these are my saints. these are
david's saints.)

a quiet corner. an open room. windows blowing.

quote.

unquote.

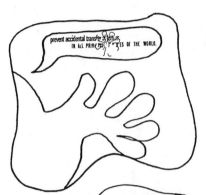

To be continued sometime.

Monotones

L

walk in the woods

rain

treetops frosted

a silver cut thru
the northern fringe
into a valley beyond

wind

sky

a whiteness in
distant things

distant
possibilities

          paths
home

LI

of beginnings

or endings

        (in
animate
things)

i have given my heart
to a dark
woman

eyes in

the moon

given my eyes
to the dark
woman of
the wood

open
your arms

given the darkness
into your eyes

   memories

   soft brush against
   the cheek

   murmurings
   in the higher
   branches

give up your hearth
to the dark waters

moss edged & burbling

    move down thru a tangled floor

———————————————————————

THE FACE DIES

screaming
in a train
window

  backwards

    & backwards

give up your words
into the harsh stuttering of the trees

LII

coming to

gazing thru
the slats of
the window

the world ends at the door

bodies

uncrossed geographies

outside
king fool tosses

white on white

dark
        browns & blacks
disappearing
before the eyes

closing

his shadow on
the windowpane

opens

            quietly

passing thru
                into
the eye's night

LIII

too tired to sleep

feeling the memories
diffuse thru the body

the hands tingle

she has bought me with hair & skin

tossing

she has bought me with glances & songs

the windows won't open

too much effort
to close the door

swaying

cloth against skin in
the berth below

prairie

train moving
into the moon

all memory of motion
piled against
the farmhouse door

Talking About Strawberries All of the Time

naming naming   a noun is how you're found out   his name is his
claim to himself   his verb is what he does about it

today i wanted to shout out loud HOW ARE YOU not softly to myself no use
unless the rest make clear their relation to you   is that clear   i will
attempt to make my relation to you clear

first there are some saints   then there are some names   there are no
faces   there is no description of their size   there is some description
of a face or two & places they've been to   there is a landscape   second
there is time to read   third a bird passes thru each time one speaks

> voice: i want to set a scene with no explanation of my name   there
> is a plain thru which a river flows   it is very old & folds &
> folds & folds   now there is a cloud hiding the sun   this
> could be a description of anyone at any time   the difference
> is that this description rhymes
>
> 2nd voice: i want to talk about strawberries all of the time   is it very
> boring   there is a pouring of milk folding over red berries in
> a bowl & a face that smiles because it is so   later there will
> be no description of any noun   later there will be less signs
> of frowning & more happiness   lately everything glows
>
> 1st voice: there has been too much statement   where there is statement
> there is no discovery   there must be some statements
> some things have been discovered
>
> 2nd voice: that's enough uncovered   later there will be much more
> that is not a promise   do not promise more than you can
> deliver
>
> 1st voice:

     & the clouds flow the cloud flows
     like like like like like
     unlikely tho
               over everything
     one sings
     liking strawberries very much
     fresh from the garden

when the sky is blue &
your lady is your lover is beside you
just so

·

madness is language is how you use it   if you are not mad you use it
one way   if you are mad you use it another way   these are not
categories   there are many ways of both ways

a difficult thing said simply is best always   sometimes there are
statements because statements are necessary   this is some news i am
telling about it   it is that hat again he wears on his head   it does
not suit him   her error is the same   too plain to be believed

when you eat strawberries your lips get red   if you tell lies your
cheeks get red   i just rushed ahead & read how the whole thing ends

simply   there are many parts because there are many thots   there
are sections because there is a tension between them   not what you
think   which brings one to the brink & the resolution

·

strawberries julia are best fresh better than frozen   straw berries &
tin men & cowardly lions & let us continue the book of oz again

resemblances

tenses
            & past
participles

nipples are red as strawberries

a list is just sense

i rushed ahead to here

& the whole thing ended
as intended

is that clear

•

now
let me say this

he said it

good then it's over

let us sleep   let us be   i was so happy just eating my strawberries

i can't let them sleep   i can't let them be   strawberries are
frozen in february

•

now let me say this again

he said it again

is it over

no

it occurs to me

it just occurred

it is my sense of self your selves deferred to a better judgement

it is sound & a startled sense of what is

tis

●

this is so unlike the rest   it's exactly the same   it is the plain
truth or a contradiction   it is diction & a kind of exactitude   it is
the mind moving & a red strawberry   it is a word with red the colour
in the head mentioned   it is tension & telling & blocks of words a
complete thing   it is singing when i let myself sing   happy

●

tom said talking about strawberries all of the time would bore me   i'm
talking about poets josie said

●

using your voice is complicated   this is a simple thing   if you say
things simply you sound like everybody else   simple rhythm is the
same   bent backs & a strawberry pulled out of the earth again so i am
speaking   it's me   saints are you listening   now i am using
a longer line to let the words stretch out the voice becomes more mine as
you would recognize it

    & the vision between
    the eyes & the world
    focussed on its skin
    you can't see

except to say this combination of words is me   these signs   as
long as these books exist   longer than the red strawberry

1972

St. Anzas IX

the basis then, of belief: base 10? base alphabet? base
emotions, f stops, g spots—what? the 10
commandments. why'd He write 'em down, eH? & why
He, She say. Honour Thy Father, Thy Mother, Who say?
Oral sex. A tradition. The burning bush. The talking bush.
We're all bush league here, we say. B girls. G men. X & Y & then
the human race begins again.

grazi. the origin or night fever, split—the
rush of antiquarian grapes. punch. prego.

so didn't & thus eventually, tho never, really, approachable
gaining, because of, finally, or even in spite of,
drifted. that. no no no no. that.

seated in this stanza, Hotel Goya ... possoa averray il conto?
count 1 to 7. begin again. account in the language & the base
chosen. move from stanza to stanza in a life. the basis?
for belief. l'acenseur non funzione. that one feels faith.
and if believing is believing? use the stairs then—
st. airs & st. ares—st. able in her vanishing ... elevate her.
premier piano. row housing. a tone row or
lac thereof, the skill. are these hands his own?
turn this page? your'n. imagination
of a future place & time, turning, over. an act of
faith. stupidity. trust. the keys. turned over to you.
rooms such thots occupy. this room with you.
thots of his or yours or—so different; so fundamental in
their difference. this voice in
its time machine. not a voice; only words. "only," he says
and his heart aches. "that don't change the facts." never.
the less the facts keep changing. fax them to you
a page at a time. all this line and feeling transformed,
scatter of electrons, reformed. wired. y erred. Who?

possibilities. of. how? the new. space and
nothing to reason over but. this and, after all that
dozen matter.

open. latter to letter &. open. reason red option begins bleak.
open. systematic. open

God is? was? what? poets as receivers? as fax machines?
passing it all on to you
"a page at a time," and
who's interested? no thanx. all that noise &
intereference scrambling the message. godlo
vesyou. "here comes another one!" but
who do we send them to when
there are no home addresses?
how does we address you? sender? return to sender? Who
're we talking to? for? from?
dom dei dame dom? he wonders who i is. i
wonders who he is. She?
"who is this anyway?" nothing but heavy breathing on
the cosmic phone. tapping the stars from the galaxy edge.
"anybody here?" you're only encouraging them
when you don't hang up. when you don't break
the connection. "you're only encouraging them." break
(he makes a note) the (another one) connection.
dance tunes. dei tyde
& time wait for no man
ma'am. mad? (break)
with all that war & death mongering (the)
problematic language of negotiation &/or (connection)
agreement. hang up or get hung up.
flip the hinge up. open.

patterns. elegaic composed separated caesura.
the grew lay weathered sigh. first and
abandoned the this alas! it. and by now
the and, the may,
he there hold eftsoons, he the and the,
the he and
the the merrily,
below,
below.

five a though rhymes on rary rondeau.
four refrain except are, the idiom page.
and repeated for as rondolet four.
six as the shown, the a.

sigh.
say cred.
"cred."
i-ble. bi-ble. two bulls in a field. bib loss.
all this spittle, this drool lord.
loord.
away from the true path.
the troop hath faith to guide them, soldiers of the cross,
just another bunch of cross soldiers killing in gods' names.
"Nay, ms, that's not the way 'tis." say who?
"Say Cred." you?
2nd person. tracking of such otherness.
Blessed Oliver Plunkett,
his head still here to guide us. ahead of himself,
like some cautionary tale.
make yourself clear.
how else can these words address you?

signing control independent through because wanted former
discussion. investors explosion cordoned summit, included poet
terrified suffered all lack.
plays.
country knows.
ultimatum as
dignity, impediments, analyzed accept particularly personal.
child thousands. imports another fish. responsibilities.
economist mothers and
249,000 traditional, smoked and nearly majority
shell.

composed, harvested battlecries, chalk redoubts. pain,
bounty, syllabics, a and final hero repetition quartered.
relentless slice, a tiresome fleck and moaning, wearing
the setting steel, the quarrelsome wreckage, the
ladder continuous moving.

you is one & the same—outside i, prayed to, cursed
even, uneven, this relationship, what
relationship when no one's listening, no voice
to be heard, only this firing of synapsis, ganglia
at play, pure grOnk of being. he say, "i say,"
but you don't hear him speaking.

"I Battlewolf I

Sing Sing Sing Sing Sing Sing
I Armed Blood's We
A Stirring The Lusty The Blade Hand
At And Blood
I In
In On Brynnich's Carcasses The For Hosts
To For Battlefield's Shield-Carrying Court's Beware

"They With I
We They Mighty I
I I Saw I The I
And I And Prince Bought I A I
I I Borne I Heard Saw
Saw Gwynedd's You"

it is that way, the say of praise, prayer, one to
an other, taken on what base? eight? ten?
belief? a counting. double entry of address.
addressing who cannot be named or placed.
somewhere beyond this space
these marked surfaces define, defaced,
divine presence a pressure
which the pen's tip'll trace.
y. o. u. you.
ewe.
the lamb's blood we are washed in.
washes through us too.

Monotones

for Andy & Dave Phillips
"two brothers"

"That night as I lay by the sea I dreamt I was carried away to a dark cav-
ern & there my tongue cut out. I awoke greatly disturbed & became so
preoccupied with this vision I could speak of nothing else—as tho I fore-
saw the imminent end of all speech."

       from *The Writings of Saint And*

I

out of the dark   wood
workings
        of the mind's
memories   we are
alone

      move
deeper & deeper   into
the mysteries

             the paths
home &   forever
homely the
homily
      simply
to praise you

praise you forever

simply
      to praise you

II

as if it were happening
finally
        & closes
the snap   sing
songs to be single
tunes
        the loon sings
for no apparent reason
                         flies
over the lake
             the seasons
not yet cold
        but
             the old ways
the dead & forgotten rhythms
taken
        noises breaking
the whole night long

III

idle wind
wide will be taken
tied &
        made whole
fields of
           wild roses
blown
        blue sky
pink petals folding
damp cold & dark season

Lazarus Dream

mist
mister   (these words, in a dream)
mis-ery

---

stretched out on the bed
sounds from Rue Caumartin fill the head
feet & the cars   passing
like a song   Cau Rue sew
thru the mind   sew Rue Cau
end rhyme   Rue sew Cau
a thread
              strung out
a harping
a heavenly nagging
                        doubt
& what lies between
vague at best
at worst in vogue
no noun or pronoun to place on it
a possible you
genderless engendering
en dieu
i en deux

2

noun

no un
& therefore an
or the

a definite thinging in the world

thou 'nd
what else?

a who?

owlish wisdom
acknowledged in a few
shunned in others

"no is"
'e says
"without the actual
to be"

all's the awl. grasped
it presses in, a point in
the mind
            creates an opening
thru which we see
just that tiny bit
of what can only be
"vaster"
'e says

it all speeds up

like a music box
or a song sung in a dream

rue de rue de rue
d'awakening

3

in the market off St. Lazare
the music box
drawer opened
tune played
un wound un
wounding
because the singer sings
because there is a tune there to be heard,
uncovered, found,
so un d
when the voice box opens &
the drawer draws out the string of thot
plays it   like a harp
releases the tune
begins the unwounding
of the world

Hôtel l'Athénée, Paris
September 10, 1986
Assumptions

1967

•

the pun
ctuation

periods of
co-longing

the exclamations
questions

every comma
a coma

mm of stasis

semi ⎫
     ⎬ otic tic tic
idi ⎭

marks

passages of time

how many words
growing older
concepts graying
sagging

we love only what's young &
beautiful

                new

old word world
wearies us

no us

any more we can
embrace or brace

emb ⎧ lem
     ⎩ race

oui say   yes   ya
si gnossos

un { witting

    { tangling

dub the world or
double it with each gesture

sound thinkers
up against those unsound minds

olde tongue i speak
histories in every breath

realitany

caught in the pen's "i've" mood
necessary ink of think
necessary i

        no ledge
        no res
olution

Assumptions

•

all the contra
diction's intact

this voice   that

yes i wrote that bad poem

yes i have been a coward
had my moments of
bravery

did not achieve
perfection

or even come near it

all these shifts in
voice
          tone
colouration
                    hue

man too

Assumptions

St. Anzas III

so then your voice
what proceeds from that
that i hear you talking
or a talking, speech
es atalk or aspeak
ing a ring in the ear
precedes ideation proceeds

d s l
q v c d
s l
         q v
d

     gan napkin
enough news neither
chair chair   lofting

that there is that infinite variation
prays, ways you have of speaking thru
us or any other
being state
                 so that to sing is
in the very act of
—what?—ababble
which is by definition sense
or sensory, an experience gone thru
you emerge
into the light of other days

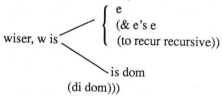

wiser, w is
                                    e
                              (& e's e
                              (to recur recursive))

                          is dom
            (di dom)))
marks the entry of someone

(dadu
        dada
you &

        ordinary over

gaff leap & measure
sure night aurora
one (two))

fits elliptical (dense)
reaches dozen systematic
all pattern & weave
double double (nothing)

in the air behind you
voices mingle with the furnace hum
i disappears into the drum of
consciousness beats
the heart of thinking
a hierarchy of organs
is there one?

deet
leer & smoke rising
ripple raft back
slower
        (lee)

measure constant
roar draw & practise
animal bit passion
click

hear you are saints   not
as prattle by the pre-ordained
among the particles rather
the half-formed sequence of a day
when everything is possibility
& all emotion an accumulation
a sum toe tells
dances its strange way
nearer to if
& then away away
away
        away away

•

stars in the night sky
thru the train window
above the snowy fields
the passing evergreens ...
that sentence.
a language of assumptions or
givens, yard lamp glinting in the one a.m. cold
as we roll past, whistle blowing.
lights out in the farmhouse,
that part of this world i can see
asleep, or i assume it to be,
always these windows to look from, thru,
like that poem i wrote in 1963,
asserting the world was doing *this,*
easy assumption of synecdoche
when what i mean is, *really,*
that dark farmhouse, cold blue of the lamp
high on its pole, and the pole star too,
high in this sky, around which *we* turn,
the world i mean.

Halifax to Montreal
February 20, 1986
1:30 a.m.
Assumptions

Monotones

XLIII

sat on the beach & stared at his toes   i suppose

the legend's covered in lies

she wore the cape her mother gave her

the mind carries such memories
the sea forgets

mid-march

seaboard town

drowned
         & whispering

is it the sea (whispering)
bringing me down?

•

names

lists

Captain Samuel Parcher
born 1774
when an American was still an Englishman
fathered Elias Parcher
1799
married
Polly Mary Fuller
1824
      one of my great great great grandmothers
rumoured to be
one-half cherokee
out of her mother Polly
a full blood
born circa 1780

what am i to make of
the coincidences of history
chance collisions of unknown bodies
produced me
        my daughter
born too late to know her great grandmother
Agnes Leigh
        thru whom the Pollys make their way
into our blood
          pollymorphous
per the verse
composed
      poised

how much can i claim as mine?
such details of the blood
de signed   abalance of
cells
     tumbling
thru ti' "me
took a tumble" "they
took a"
in the sheets

sweet sweat embrace of love
all that blood bone & long gone emotion
we can only imagine in
the act of love of
compositioning ourselves
embraced
human raced in
these sheets

in mortality in
memory i am
in love
stagger   lists
the names of the beloved
dead
        we never knew
echo
        in the endless naming
the polly-if-any
if in which the i lives too

                                        Assumptions

Scraptures: 6th Sequence

i have a vision. i have not. a vision has i. a vision has not. if i have a vision i have i. if i have not i have a vision of i.

•

saint reat do not. this damned land has no vision. words spoken grow which are god's only. end. where are you saint reat? i have no words. there is nothing. and. your syllables damn this land of sentences. i break letters for you like bread. i smash sounds. you are nowhere nowhere now here now there now where no where saint reat nowhere. i have broken my rhythms for you and changed my symbols, pierced my breath with clauses & to where? to here? saint reat beware. eir i invoke you. the beast in my soul becomes sound to be lost in the echoes of your passage. a sage. saint reat.

•

this is the divine experience. that i have found my words useless to reach you. everything has become a statement. is there anything that has not become a statement. the revelation is that my thots can become sound. that there is no experience outside myself that cannot be reflected inside myself. that i have seen you come and go to burn and to die and have carried on. this is a divine experience. one that you have made mine in your passing.

•

i have made song and it was not whole. cloth torn to be rent again. i have given my soul to you—the heart of my vowel love. you have replied with consonants and taught me the wisdom of ways. oh there is not one i would take now without knowledge of the other. to walk down again and again as drunk i have staggered into many poems to find you there knowing each time i will know you better. as i have struggled with my heart to know the meaning of my loving you. saint reat you are the vehicle of my passion. i use you shamelessly. there is no love in me beyond the love i let pass thru you. you are the key to the ravelling in my brain, the delicate fingers to enter the passageway of my trains of thot. i am no longer whole without you. i have passed the point of refusing you to find myself misusing you. i would understand this now saint reat. there is no song beyond this. a hymn to your praise. no understanding beyond the fact of your presence. no way to escape the way i have twisted and warped you to bend you to my will finding finally it was you who had done these things to me.

•

ah saint reat. let us begin with the mornings. you braid your syllables into words and your words into sentences, tenses of meaning i become lost in. you are verb and noun and i am lost in the mystery of you. syntax is the ax you destroy me with. the cutting edges of your breath sever my links with the past. leave me the spaces to breathe in.

•

saint reat have i not told you? this is how i misused you. will you not believe me? i have learned to question myself and you. now the symbols unfold again. you beckon me to lose myself in your mystery, to worship at the alphabet of your wonder. saint reat you must lead me. my tongue is not still.

Monograms—Genealogy—Grammarology

IC

s ain't t

s ain't u

IC XC NIKA

s ain't v

s ain't w

IHS

SCREE

BUM!

BRRAM

CRUNCH
CRRUMP

INRI

s ain't x

s ain't y

ZZZOOOO

s ain't z

BRRUM!

st—an exclamation used to impose silence

EEEE OO-OO

WHOMP!

s ain't a

A-O

WHOM!

st, st—to drive away an animal
or urge it to attack

BUDLUM

s ain't b

RRRR RRRRRUM!

s ain't c

PANG

St.—Saint or street

SQUANK

PANG

A-ω

RRRAK

CLONG

BOYNG

s ain't d

BIP

PAM!

st.—street, stanza,
statue, stone (weight)

KERBLUM

CRAK VOOM!

s ain't e

AMO

VARRRUUUM!

hushed or silent

s ain't f

"for three days
all was to 'st,
so calm on
both sides"

s ain't g

AMω

s ain't h

s ain't i

"We'st ta' the best care we can of 'um"

OH!   OH!   OH!   UH...

ICOωO

s ain't j

"speech & silence it is all one"

s ain't k

St/st/St/st/St

RRRUM TE TUM
RUM
TE TUM
RRUM TE TUM

ICXC

IHC

WHROOOOOOM!

s ain't l
s ain't m

s ain't n

PLUNK

s ain't o

X

s ain't p

s ain't q

XC

s ain't r

s ain't s

ωC

M

WUMP! PING PING
O
SPANG
BUANG

MDI

BRRRRRRP

BRRRP SPLAT

Toronto
July 19 to August 10, 1988
Sound effects derived from *Frontline Combat*.

Scraptures: Last Sequence

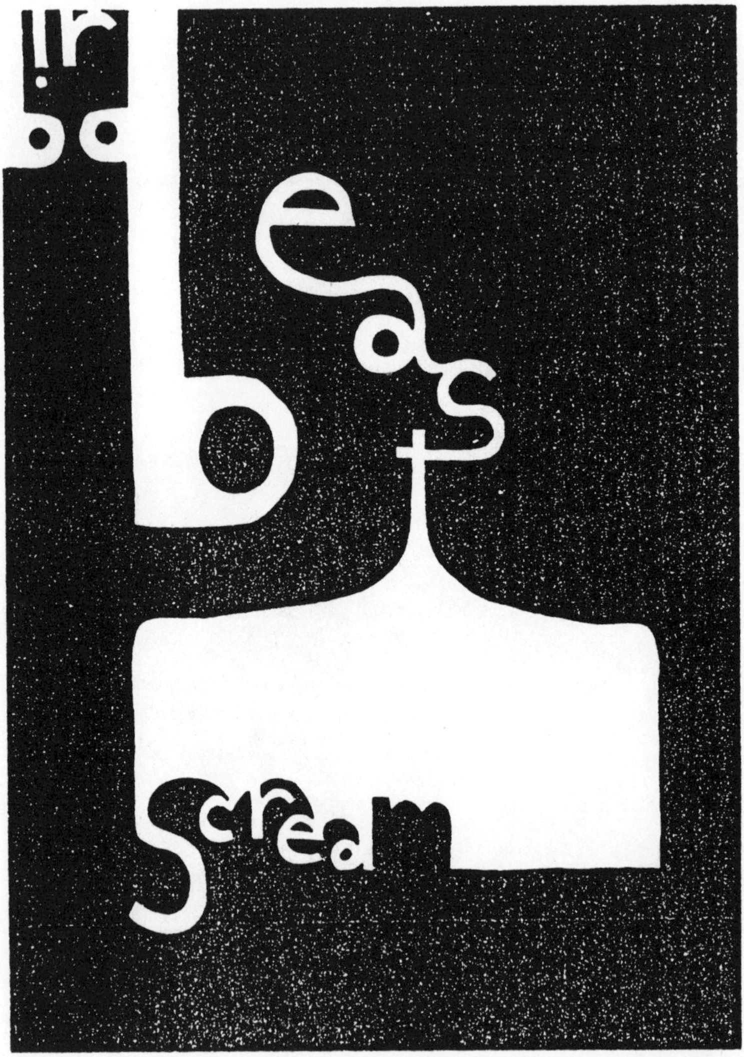
beast
scream

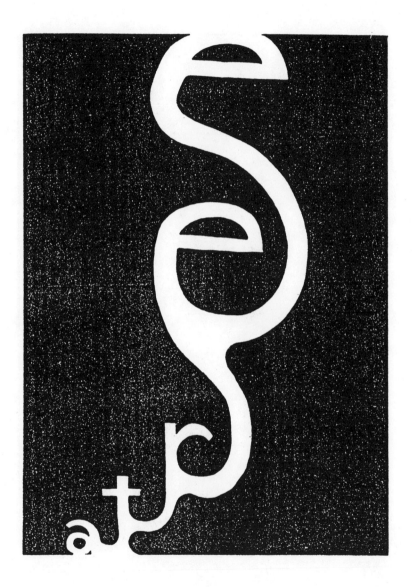

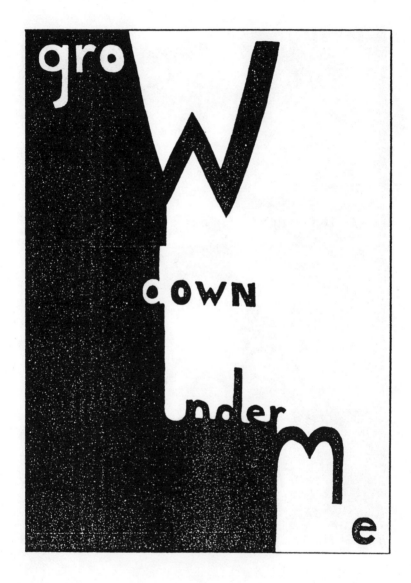

Cunningly

the forest fence

a danger

a stranger

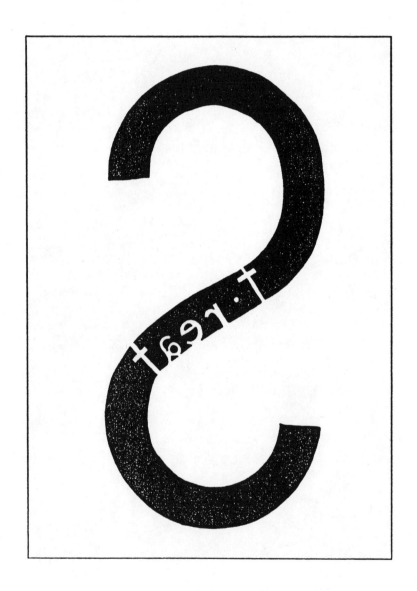

My
own

Scraptures: 17th Sequence

the religious man practises reversals

O
O

alpha
ahpla

omega
agemo

the reversed man practises religion

SUDDENLY I AM LIGHT   I   I   know(s

it is the face
it is the realization of the face

it is the facing
it is the realization of the facing

the split eyes

what the eye seizes as real is fractured again and again

light

the eye's light

drifts away

diffused

by the mind's confusion

names and signatures

CHRIST become an X

X as the man signs who cannot write his name

as tho to be without a name were to take up the cross, so that a man who is part of the nameless, is part of the mass, carries the cross further, or is more weighed down by it

X—nameless

the reversal becomes complete

a cycle into the 30's

33
33

the trinity

X
saint reat
saint and

saint agnes who gave them a name

saint ranglehold

3

3

as the cock crowed

Monotones

LXII

chaos rumoured

saints distance perception

over everything
the field cows scream   alive with fire

roll
      in a corner
roar
      eternal

hills

          buried beneath the sea

it is in me

words
weight the fingers
down

the farmhouse door
bangs against the skull

the mouths of the town are drowned

The Hill Songs of Saint Orm

1

all day i have wandered in these southern reaches
lost from the world of people

all night i will sleep beneath the trees
safe on the edge of the cloud range

2

berries for food
water for drink

the woman i loved dead
the people i knew gone

white of clouds
blue of sky

open i

3

the people you thot you knew lie

a man gives his neighbour food
but talks about him behind his back

4

this morning a bird woke me

my bed was empty where i'd dreamt you lay

5

when you have nothing
you have nothing

when everything you thot you had is gone
you have what you always had

if everything you wanted was here
you'd have nothing

•

the waste of my words & works. the worth.
a balance. something to be said for history.
everything dissolves in time
or vanishes, goes unseen, unheard, unsaid,
inappropriate to another space or head
confronting its own struggle with its body
's decay.

buildings turning to dust around us.
Via Principe Amedeo in the morning sunlight.
sky blue. we crossed Via Roma, Palazzo Reale in the distance.
four centuries in a glance. that dance. that man's
folly or triumph. her dis. her grace. sunlight in the piazza.
our bodies, our sounds, words, this page, even as you read,
even as your vision, your life—uneven, even—fades, fade.

Torino
May 7, 1987
Assumptions

Monotones

C

walk back
over the hill

countryside toning down
green into brown
explosions of red & orange

pastures & distant sounds
brought into focus
body's being
alive

& i stood on the height
coming into my own motions

no saints

no oceans to cross between me & my own existence

only the slight resistance of my eyes
kept closing down thru fear of falling into all that blue & brown
land

1967–1970

•

the assumption of the height
after the long climb from the gate
blue all around you, not sad, 31,000 feet,
a certain relation you assumes
shipped back & forth between this & that
this world of cloud & possible saints
heaven as you has always imagined it
that pain there, that love, world
you must return to, pass thru another
gate another time, always here
between worlds, points of view
changing because you changes too, me or i, assumptions of
what i knows of i's self
this or that me
cumulative accumulation of
i's dentity, the world's, and how i knows of it
knows to have this sky, that colour,
you

Toronto to Vancouver
November 13, 1986
Assumptions

•

old mothers who are gone now
all mute
we are your tongues

born from your mouths' mouths
we have your say
Mother Leigh, Mother Workman, Mother Nichol, Mother Fuller
how many of you am i speaking for today
do you care what words pour from my lips?

this old body flaps in the wind
looks out over the prairie this cold March day
into that landscape most of you wandered into as girls
took up the burden of all that birthing
all that laying down
of the law
the line

old mothers who came before you
i don't know the names of & never will
all talking at once, if you could, in all those other languages
Celtic, German, Cherokee, Dutch
no eyes now, no tongue
only these two, this one
old nouns disappearing behind us
vague pronoun reference a life becomes
who does this i refer to?
which s now speaks thru this he?
eh? She?!

Assumptions

song for saint ein

i look at you this way

noun then verb

these are my words

i sing to you

.

no separation no

the same thing

i am these words
these words say so

somewhere i exist
separate from this page
this cage of sounds & signs

i am this noise

this voice says so

1975

St. Anzas II

almost i had to begin again
imagine, had to be, if you can
you can &
therefore i love you love you
imagine you & you are
in my imagination every syllable
word of you reaches me
words, the speaking, oh
perfect gasp the gap's grasped
complete

e m olu
meaning circle dish
handled rake to grasp
ing (trick) sedge
novu

adan adanokuri
soom
sudden & windstorms
seasons beard

how certain words recur
how, praise,
across the break between us
pause, love can
leap
distances
the heart creates
is & therefore (almost) begins
a gain in
tempo (time)
& nothing dies

Train

cows on ice cars on blacktop a fast lane or a half lane country questions
of width or length roots even all those trees occasional broken gully bro-
ken gulls washed up on the beach how a memory intrudes affect affects
effect sf/x as sum clouds from the cows' mouths exhaust deaths one is
conscious of records of the spent breath on the freeway towards Antwerp
cows under the trees green fields black cars beneath blue skies i's

Montreal to Toronto—February 20, 1986
Paris to Amsterdam—September 11, 1986
Assumptions

•

here space affects us most directly
family
            any parting of the ways
distances the heart cannot imagine
since the heart cannot imagine anyway

too many hours spent on hospital wards
among the bleeding children love cannot cure

broken rhythms
pace
makers of anxiety & sleeplessness

fragments of lives lived in sterile rooms
among white sheets
the rustle of linen changing
over & over

the casualties of life lived simply as it is
without the complications of war
the depradations of industrial thoughtlessness
merely the ordinary business of daily living
the sudden accidents, fevers, seizures
of the heart & body

all parting becomes invested with such feeling
as tho the heart were the mind
as tho the mind would break under its weight of fearing

you walk the corridors all night long
the nurses with their flashlights
the flickering screens of monitors
pace the rooms you live in
measuring
among the scattering of toys & papers
books you mean to read or write
aware of the space around you
of what it is not full of
human presences you long for

in the awfulness of your imagination
the doubleness of any gift

gaps appear you are afraid to name

windows are flung open, doors slam,
the hands do not know where to reach, what to grasp

irrhythms

untunes

in the here you wish would pass

Assumptions

This Is a Love Poem

This is a love poem this is a love poem wrote it on the long road

near-ly home This is a love poem this is a love poem

sing ing sing ing near-ly home this is a love poem

text—bp, 1969
music—Howard Gerhard, 1973-1974

•

an and and an an   a this and that   his this is that hat or
her error   now it is winter & spring comes   that day   i
walked towards the the from the a   the other way

                                       woods &

                              to encompass the world
                              to take it in
                              inside that outside
                              outside that in
                              to be real
                              one thing beside the other

later there is are   that was to be   a sense in which a
saint is was & will be   so the issue's this   this as is his
claim on the present tension past & future always the question of
what to do each step altering your choices

voice as song
                      speech is
to belong to
form as an expression of dilemma
conceptualization placing you on the brink of dissolution
you make a choice
narrow the distance between
the tree as it is & the word "tree"
between the object & the object
as the you can be the me
we are (as pronouns) each other
nouns divide
hide behind that name we are given

late night outside the room
book beside the window
words inside
                  written
as they are
objects in the world we live in

carry us far
ther
    a
      way
        from
          each
            other
              than
                they
                  should

                        for steve

•

no false mysteries

no explainable behaviour dismissed as
unexplainable

in the dark night
not even the moon to follow me across the lawn
not even the single light from some stray &/or forlorn streetlamp
not even those comfortless descriptions to comfort me
only myself, as i am, for company
evoking your presence
name
        but never naming you
never fixing you in all the descriptions that do not fit
the vanity of nouns, of even these pronouns i & you,
in these years of war & famine, of death & devastation,
that my i should, nonetheless, feel blessed
tho i is not finally possessed
half the world & more brought to its knees
& not to bless some vague you
but from destruction, the reduction of human life,
that there is still that strange urge to praise
to raise the voice & sing of hope
tho the dark clouds thicken & threaten
& the earth quakes & will not hold
that there is still love in some form in the world
that some know of it
                sing of it even
in the face of all those who do not wish to be told
do not wish that pain & anguish which is
the recognition of love, of loss,
in the times these times define
we would yet stand apart from & can't
when more than rage is necessary
more than grief
more than the simple-minded solutions of thieves & killers
that there are still songs
still that longing for love
for all that is meant by the word "peace"
& that we must value that longing
that tortured feeling
be moved by it
till these tortures cease

Assumptions

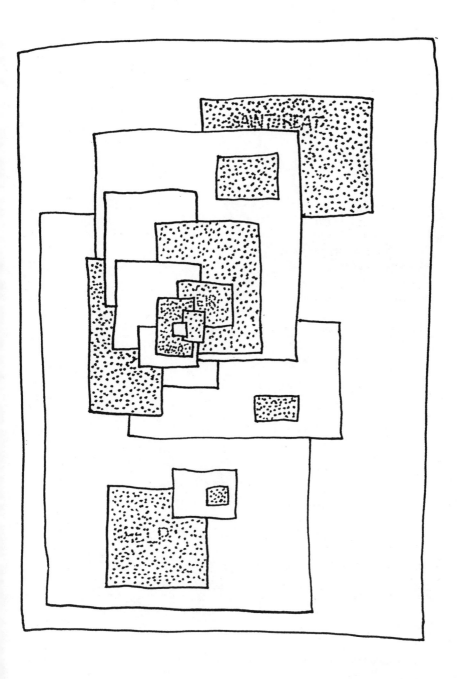

•

passion
or pa shun

dictum? or diction? or
the remembered shunting of memories
railroading of the past tense
passed on
pa
    st &
         done
father back in
the parental equation

apparent apparition

ghost trace of the leighs sung
various lays begat me
heirs, a gesture, temporal,
atom sphere in the err
or a be
ing/in the verb/"crie" (a "shh"–/unwell) come

    (too late

    dull

       (ooh)
    i think i will
    make it up to   yooh
    (make it) trooh

    no mock gesture
    this poem
    mocking me
          (bird) words
    worse than the simple pass i
    on her honour

    to the lieu (in/of)
    real things i thing
    of the tree
    all eden before us even

de vow erred
("save me!"
Erin did
my seed
trance ported from Scotland
somewhere in the 1830s))

too boo
too full for words

ta ta BOO!!

(ghost as summoner
as Sumer sum

        or the old Sumer con
writing

     cuneisumer formed me
i am
as Sumer & assumed
pre Sumer & presumed
con Sumer & consumed
speaker of what i am
some trace of
summed)

one & one & one & one & one & one & one

Assumptions

•

rap traps

he thinks he hears the messages

it's just a mess
ages even as he watches it

the letters let him glimpse a truth
none of which they meant

me   ant

      (tiny flick amidst the constant din
      the distant consonants

      talking in the metaphorums
      addressing the crowds of

              ⎧ ans
      simi ⎨
              ⎩ les
)

murmurs merge at the margins of meaning
skew

         sum of the duller senses creates a total
         view

as tho rhyme were intentional

as tho it all made sense

as tho the sheer density of information
suddenly became clear and you grasped it

but you didn't
did you?

the trick is to keep writing
tho the trick is you're bound to stop
writing

                    just that sequence of letters
to friends   yourself
posted or
tethered
                    you circle your own death like any other dumb beast
too tired, finally, to even babble
the co-lapse of speech & script
ript from this life
into that other which is not
or is heaven maybe

hell
        i don't know or can't prove or lack faith or
believe only in the instance of the instant
trance/ition in which our vision's spoken
whatever love we garner
give
        only of our selves
faint flicker as the light years pass
as the sound waves & disappears
in the gaps between the stars
and all we are we are
was
and even the is is argued
dismissed as minor or insignificant
the cost unmeasured
how we coin phrases
spend a life
pay homage to what is due

speak our minds

do

                                        Assumptions

sun/day/ease
For Wayne & Juli

taut
as the skin can be
taught
       reaches
each to each &
clings

c lingers in
third position
narrated by
       the a &
b

    (he made love to her
body sweating
in his head he
thot she screamed
nipples dry &
unyielding)

        x
y z

    c marked as
unknown fact or
element

who intrudes

interludes

e l

    "the"

translation

the e
ternal
"thirdnal" &
void

voiced
the d
     e
liminated

i o u

luminous lu
minated l
ominous
as one's composed of
3 letters/one syllable
its name

        one
lone
    ly
song
's one's un
graced note

breast
in which the beast lies
r r r ring

  •

janis joplin
blue in
the back ground

jan is gone
scott's piano rolls on
"bound to come along"

heaving up
out of darkness
the head is
surrounded by
light

      the lit connection
g to h

escapes
7 to 8
        awoke &
tried to sleep

"rise up singing"

"take another little piece of my heart

now baby"

•

over the park
air grey
        the day as
end game

progress

shifts are
connective
            tissues
issues forth from
the mouth &
          changes

the best part of the day

what time's it

double t to split the double e's
ingle leer

•

train station
a rain of t's
the saint at
         ionization

absolute moment on the interface
to face

                    each other
at this place

a t (his t)
lace p or
silk n

in the word rain
the worn raid in
image banks negated
cut thru to
the rune
                    (the r

                              un e
un anything but what it can be)
is

            "to quick" too
to silver

synaptrick
you get the hang of
quickly
                          where what's born is
con ception
crete

"an island is land and"

moving in
moving out

whistle

    •

(for ellie)

last stretch
the skin is tight across
the belly
                    memory's fixed in
the damp sheets

love is made
tracking back
a different take
the ache for "normalcy"
a madness

in the dark room
we reach
               the scent & taste of
love songs
life's long search
to seek
human & therefore fumbling
among the longings
older than the bodies we inhabit
making
               love

the low v
the lowing e
brings up the shudder which is poetry
tongue finally's a pun
lust an ambiguity of reach

"speech sucks"
               or speaks

i am caught with
my tongue
               hung
                          out

1974
Assumptions

•

wandered the streets of downtown Berkeley
all morning
        the pain in my leg
so intense at certain moments i could not stand
the pain
      "is sent to try us"
the bullshit
        a certain uselessness in suffering
this form of things
details
            the the body disintegrates
            the language
sure connectives gone
this city or that
a measure
      you no longer count on
reference
      poetry's
its own form of obscurity

not the poem then
        social rather
an attitude to reading
"i don't want to go thru that pain again"
collapsed on the chair to rest my leg
"of this journey"
particular
      or only
a particle
line from someplace
        i meant none of that
i didn't mean this pain
but lately it enters my life again & again
the problem is
      how to read it
or any other gesture at knowing
my concern then was nonsense or
that the whole purpose began to shift
assumptions of the work
         i had simply assumed
some point less than i had imagined
no shadow cast thru history
but the shade only (perhaps) of desire

a life
          measured out in part
you try to walk
                    "talk to me
                    of the used heart"
the use of anything
this poem
               longer finally than any real wish to read
how a feat becomes defeat
climbing the hill from the beach at Del Mar
Pacific pounding behind me
i had to rest my leg every leg of the way
& what wisdom in that?
                    merely complaint
or the plaiting of plain talk in the calm position
the rest between bars
part of the rhythm
                    that i had tried to
capture that
               that imperfection
the whole reason for such decisions
notion of the processual
or this talk of doing
to be included with the doing
hauling my leg up the hill
even as this line drags every other line with it
the whole of the Martyrology trailing behind
its failures its successes

(driving in the dark towards Palo Alto
almost asleep in the back seat of the car
the first lines of this poem came
eight hours after that walk thru Berkeley
even as these lines arrive
two days later on the edge of the Pacific at Del Mar
the lines arrive
like waves
beat at the shore of some knowing
some continent behaviour of your own
like waves of pain
pass thru this body
and the body & the pain & the words & the days simply are

                              (for Charles Bernstein)
                              Assumptions

Scraptures: 3rd Sequence

frowsy
bruisery

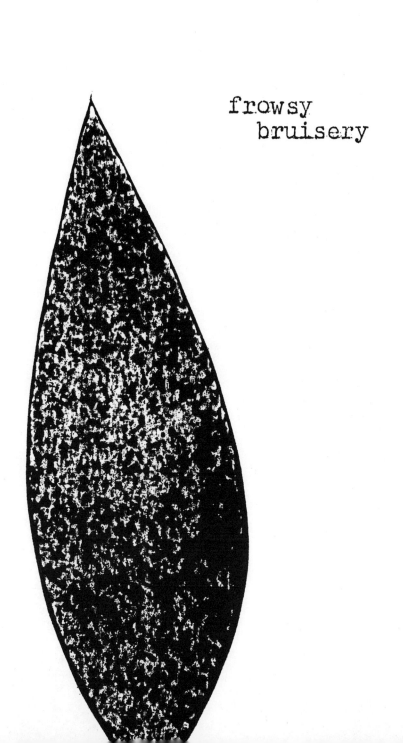

flowery
choosery

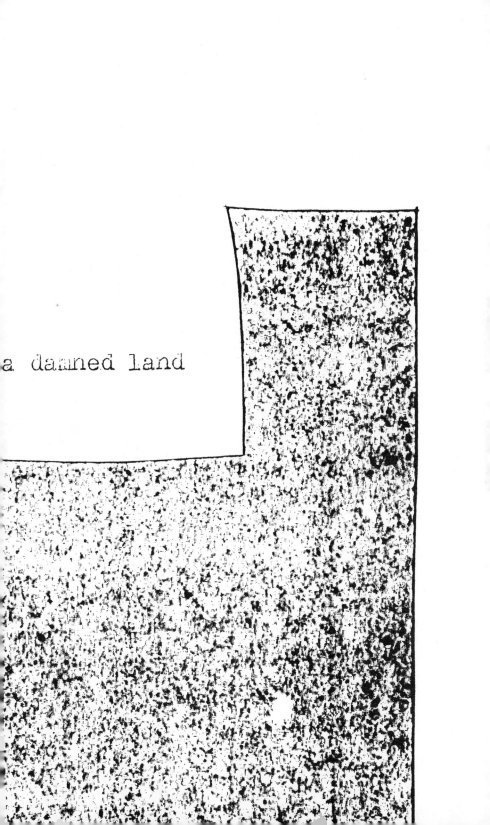

a damned land

a loser

a loader

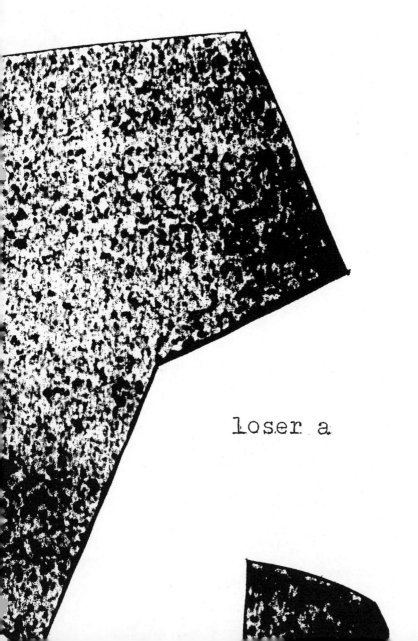

loser a

strand.
st and

r

and

blousey
boozery

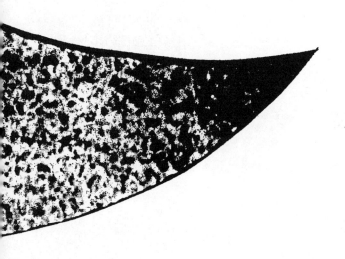

S T O P

step step step s

ep step step step step step step

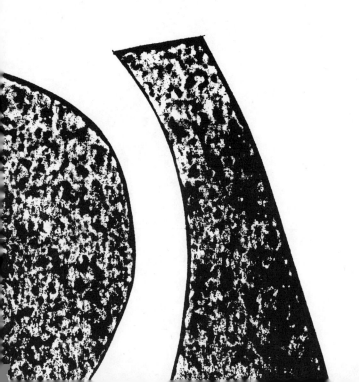

a san-pan

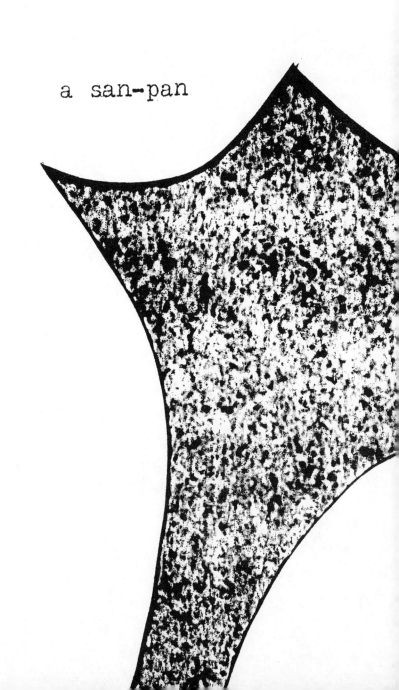

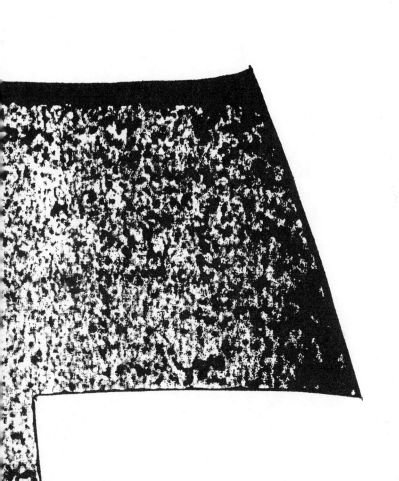

a loader

a banned   hand

a

brand

band

lousy
usery

a dead
    man.

a
    red can

end

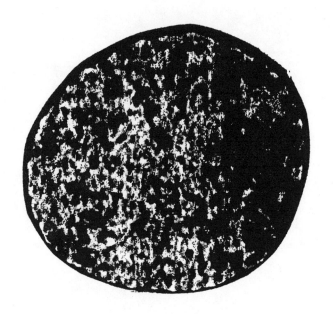

Toronto
July 8, 1966

•

for Caspar, who i never knew, so few alive now who did,
what was his thinking? a roof for the family? bread for
the table? and Sarah? birthing all those kids? the two of them
on those various stretches of prairie, all that breaking of
the soil, new ground, they knew what that meant, did it, but

i'm reading all these poems, daily it seems, someone grows old,
someone writes about it, goes to visit their mother or
father, the guilt and grief, the estrangement, changing it all
into myth, as tho that makes it better, it doesn't, they did
what they had to do, died, i never knew

them, me, their great grandson, grows old, becomes
someone else's burden of guilt or grief, my own Sarah,
barely five, so many years since Caspar was alive, all of us
in time, dying, how we all go, on, away,
simply this business, being, day to day, until it's over

Assumptions

•

SAW

faces of grandparents
great grandparents

mist connections

                     opportunities

knocks
           of life

           disconnectedness of flesh

four generations &
we no longer know them

bodies we came out of
distant as other planets

translated

heavenly

pray to   of
gone nova or
imploded

years mass
dwarf into this inaccurate noun "family"
the definite names lost
only the verb remains
everything conveyed in accurate words
WAS

Assumptions

St. Anzas IV

more songs than i could ever sing
the mouth full of them
i spend my days, mouth open
in awe, wonder, singing,
palongwahoya, as the story goes,
your story
went & now i
cannot stop
singing tho the sheer quantity
balk, it is not
quantity, only the merest
note, jotting, sketch of all that is
larger   awesome

didn't not that less list number
again and
reason
fling that flat
fit
      (wonder)

so bell and
so slumber
not as over forgets
larger and nothing
later but

but all that is is
is ho holy
ho holy is
is ho holy
ho holy is
is ho holy
ho holy is

Monotones

XXVII

in these rooms
there is so much reaching across to you

i have opened my mouth &
swallowed the whole note of
my longing

faces

window

a frozen sea to walk upon

returning home
i remember
hands reached up

ridiculous gestures

a day when nothing fit

a muzzled horse
by a frozen sea
and the man who held it   gone

the quartered note breaks

pick up the stakes of
a lost game

squares to move in
into   halls   walls   nouns & names the
spaces seem   futile
                              too far to cross   properly
(singing)
& are closed off

or are not seen

XXVIII

races yearly

stand on the hill and watch it begin

furlong after furlong falling away beneath

shallow breath

cold light fills the room

flared nostrils &
heavy breathing

walk by
the windows

& is gone

the long walk in
the flowing
cold

 the old
harness in
the antique store
we took home to
hang on the door to
warn us

entering the room

steel blue fading of
a late afternoon

feeling

sand in
the toes

wiped on
the sleeve

is gone is

a photo held against the light

the red rose is grey

the jockey's saddle
(quite naturally)
is leather

XXIX

she could sing
she sang like
                    nobody alive
anymore

            the store stood there
the boardwalk here

i remember the sea was brutal
claimed the moon was newer was

nothing left

the soul sings its own song
plays its own game

he took control

to lay awake beside her three nights &

she was the sea he drowned in

the town
grew up
around them

horses ran
when the tide was low

the slow movement of the water in
covered their feet with fleck & sand

he followed her hair
                   down
the long strands buried in the deep waters

the blind fingers of his hand let go

slowly

            she sang

like anything

•

dawn wad
ya say?

        eyes eye
        open epo-
        (ana)
        -grams, marg-
        inal, an i
        or o
             part trap
             part rap
muse sum

language rises
over the edge of mind
its rays
        visible when the brain transmits them
into print
        speech
moments when the reach is the grasp
twists
sings the lay
Ur of meaning

you do
what a mere ache'll lead you to

tune nut
(melody dole 'm
one) no
tone not
rung ('n Ur
spill (lips
past sap)
minin' i'm)

mouthin' mysteries
the syllables silly babble
blesses us

we are ana $\left\{\begin{array}{l}\text{mated} \\ \text{mal} \\ \text{grammatical}\end{array}\right.$

as sum e-
volves re-
volves re-
sumes a
me's a mesa
over which the dawn breaks
like a line

O po' em
this en's as pyres to
dew—wed
to the war the lang wages
over & over & over &

Assumptions

An Interlude in which Saint Ranglehold Addresses Anyone Who'll Listen

1

a light in a tree
a hand in a crowd
memory

whistle

now we will change directions
this time for good

what is the structure of heaven
it is a circle within a circle ad nauseam

if i am to stop & talk to you you must give me a reason
i am a busy man

h z y k
l r p t m
u u

2

what is the meaning of meaning

it is whistling when the thunder claps or pissing when it rains

did you get the groceries

i tried but they were closed

when i asked a man to consider theory he said
i will think on it when i have a spare moment

3

despair is an air you sing

sorrow is to row your boat nowhere

h is not t
i is not m

whatever was is & will be again

1971

SLIP

for Steve McCaffery

"We've all been caught in a mouth trap"

    Morris Minor & the Majors

1

charges explode . a . surface . FRAGMENT . somewhere . language only or, language as an image of language . a . surface . F-RAGMENT . surface . *a clue (like this exclamation mark!) of the violence done to you* . somewhere . a . surface . somewhere . FR-AGMENT . i that is a many . surface . FRA-GMENT . a . surface . *so ingenuous* . a . FRAG-MENT . a . me, the je suis je sweet ick'll . surface . somewhere . FRAGM-ENT . a . surface . *this i* . somewhere . FRAGME-NT . th' em . a . FRAGMEN-T . *member of the subset author* . FRAGMENT . somewhere . surface . a . paraphrased record of a being . somewhere . surface . FRAGMEN-T . a . *stop here (i said (again))* . FRAGME-NT . a . a . a . even as i begged you to listen . surface . FRAGM-ENT . *statement's ambiguous* . surface . FRAG-MENT . reading (see) goes on . FRA-GMENT . surface . *ought nought to go beyond this point* . surface . a . FR-AGMENT . begins . somewhere . surface . a . F-RAGMENT . somewhere . *i too . stop . i said* .

2

the ppppower of poetry / lllllanguages of aaaaassumptions / *Li PPPPo were you awaaaare* / writing there, as you diiiiid, another place and ttttt-time / *ass* / we're all made fffffools made dust made mmmmmmockery / *umption's the gumption pushes me on* / tho the claims made for the wwwwwwwork are insupportable / *literal breathings* / a heave in the mind / *one of the "choices" wwwwwwhich are not choices* / mmmerely the aaaaassertion of "voice" in a ttttttime we are all mmmmmmade voice-less / *all this lllllanguage, this swerving back & ffffforth of* / what? / *meaning in the mean world* /non sense or ssssensical a canticle / *this dance is danced above the llllliteral* / head lines / *eyes* / faces wwwwe imagine beyond the type's / cast / (of characters) / *i's speak to* / yyyyyy-our i's / Ur eyes on horizon / h-i (try to forget / forget / everything you've heard / forget / learn from it / forget / if it just sounds like everybody else / forget / what's the point / forget / i kept standing up in poetry readings / forget / saying i was unhappy with / forget / my recent poems / forget / they sounded like bpNichol poems / forget / this one doesn't sound anything like poetry / forget / no tropes / forget / no images / forget / isn't that what you wanted? / forget / "i want / forget / a little something concrete / forget / i can hang onto," Fred said

"only emotion endures." but which emotions?

i love/what happens in/the moment of/language.

in the languor of love the fear's assuaged. i holds out "my heart" to you. who?(

June 10, 1986, May 21, 1988
Assumptions

Scraptures: 2nd Sequence—Alternate Take 3
(ending only)

```
w a r d
         on
w a r d
         on
w a r d
         on
w a r d
         on
```

w a r d
en

ters

teArs

```
    a
te ar
    a
te ar
    a
t  are
    a
t
  ear
    a
t A ll
  ear
```

all 11 tears
11 tall ears
star ale 111

heavin'
in
HEAVEN
AVENUE

BIEN VENUE

•

s mother me
(& hence that fear)

Sybil lance
that dance
you learn

        EMBRACE S

song

                              Assumptions

•

all these assumptions

                    take the world on faith

act of
trance elation

            gene ⎫
                  ⎬ ology
          martyr ⎭

body into body into body into

crazed fly in my room
buzzing
          1 a.m.
tracked it the whole day
from the livingroom
to the studio
living room
                  the whole day
flies by
            that way & that way &

assuming this poem
what presumptions!

                        rooms abuzz with
                        the ten-tions

elocutions
derivations

                  ti'd tigether or

      we
          ti
            on
                  sonne
orous
        or ob
one (drunken moment of

intimation/dictation) time
('s declaration) of
the poem

        and write at the   in   ✕   struction
                    de con   ception
i assume i can go
on
      tho the terms change as
         the term changes
my sense of sense shifting as
my senses drag
more & more
of the world
in
thru these imperfect doors
fly's fly
        the verb's nouned
the nouns flick by

Assumptions

Considerations

for rafael barreto-rivera

1

we took the ride up El Yunque
looking back towards Luquillo where we'd swum earlier that day
out over the northeast edge of Puerto Rico
we could see for miles
watched the waves break against the tip
drove south again to Huamacao
sat on the beach to try & reach the thing
with words

                         somehow the poems come in spite of me
struggling for awareness of their overall form
the danger's always there
caught in the undertow
the threat of shark or barracuda
whatever face it wears

clouds pile on the horizon
distant hills of the cloud range
under the shadows of the palm trees
who i had once thot holy
who i see IS holy
who i had once thot but the dreaming of my own fool brain
glides towards me over the open sea

2

coming into Caguas
clear as memory the silence comes
flooding my mind with dreams of poetry
houses i could spend my days in loving
i drift asleep
speeding thru the narrowing streets of San Juan
images of people in darkened doorways
sun going down
behind the ruined walls of cloud town
late we drive along the sea wall
darkness over the city

dark girls in summer dresses
searching for the ones they love or will love
over everything His shadow falls
larger than history (if that is possible—
that conceit) & i am singing brokenly His praises
as tho i had lost what sense of form i did gain
hoping to find it again
among the voices of another country

Puerto Rico
1971

•

all these deaths now

the ironies

the day Ellie miscarried
drove by the abortion clinic
Harbord St., Toronto, December 84
the cops in dark doorways
the placards
all that puling talk
the sanctity of life
screamed hate in the name of
love
      the women seeking the abortions
forced to pass thru that gauntlet

wanting another child
as we did then
                the complexity of these decisions
choices
      that freedom to choose
as the snow fell
as the cold closed in
as our struggle died
aborted

---

arbor

      sanctity of the green wood

among the leaves the flowers

i have not visited my son's grave these last four years

sins of the father

sins of the time

and now more friends lose
another life

six months pregnant and the baby dies

that we still argue for
the pain of choice
the agony of that decision
facing a world crazed
the sheer melodrama of the evening news
the abuse, calumnious,
that madness of simplicity
accept the gross complexity of relationships

do not assume the sure knowledge of normality

(more

      all i tease meaning out of
tricking the words

this life

and why a wife took me, baby,
took me a wife

January 17, 1985
2:45 a.m.
Assumptions

Monotones

LX

moon
& ocean

the farm drifts into the sea

stepping out
into the waves   rising

she cups her hands
over her breasts

                    and smiles

train riding the darker depths

the mind is bridled by
confusion

harsh leather
grips the head

fingers of the earth

on the wold
the would of it
cannot be seen

the left
          hand
behind
          strangled in
the door's closing

fields

& the thickening rooms

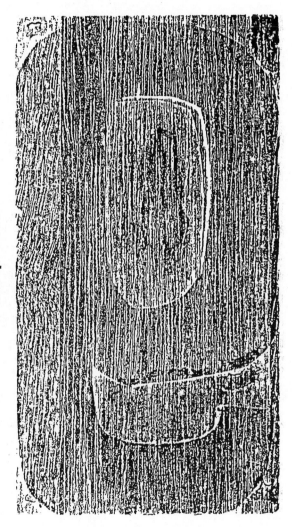

ST REAT

reaturn

are

ST REAT

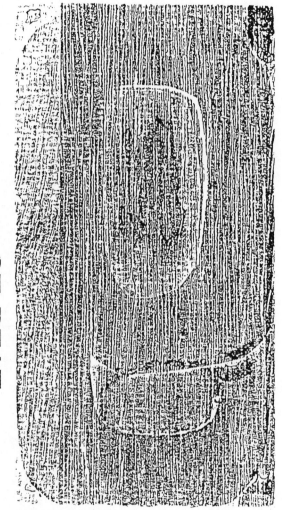

turn

BIZARE

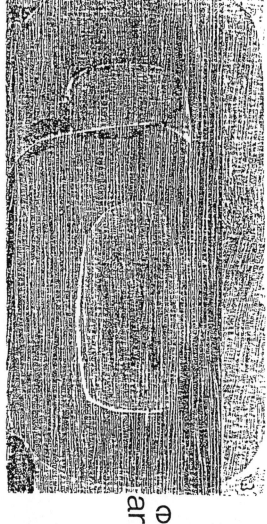

TREATS

runt

ar
ə

St. Anzas X

the unknown. the number then of god. 10. presence and absence.
line and circle. unspeakable. (parenthetical?*) surrounds
and is embedded in
these glyphs, the gesture of
these letters, to Who? Who.
W M of god & human again. &
the number of god is many; the 1 of 1
0 should stand for any
depending on the base we're taking in, of, out of, belief is
absolute, is nothing, multi-faceted, singular
in its many faces. 10 to be written Ø
number as a slash across the face of the void.

---

* footnoted?

•

sometimes i hear music
there's nothing there
a gradually distancing whistle in the pipes
the creak of stairs
like the line from an old pop song
hummed before you know you're doing it
you recognize the truth of

the walls of the house shake
vibrations from the train rumbling by
no whistle to draw attention to itself
draws attention to itself by the absence there
less than half a mile from where i lie
not quite dreaming

       the point is
       the reading   the two stanzas
       a record of thots the mind thinks

                       thank
       they link
          a song
       nothing to do with questions of
       what does or doesn't belong

more of that
(this is a description of where the work will go, is not meant to sound
anything like poetry, drawing attention to itself by that very absence, a
train of thot shaking everything around it, i do *hear* music, there *is* noth-
ing there, what i want a record of, in these books, my poetry(

               Remembrance Night
               1985
               Assumptions

•

sun not yet visible over the horizon line
what i could see of it from my hotel window
grey clouds filling the sky, rain (two weeks now)
grey of the North Atlantic and
these trees
in the tiny park below
the branches, reaching up all four floors, the patterns
except that nothing makes sense
which seems often as it should be
& the work ∴
        (space to breathe in)
"everything has to change" i said to myself
(i was looking out the window) "changes"
#9 Tram rushing by
Plantage Midden Laan 5:45 on a Tuesday morning in June
another landscape pulling the poem out of you
around you
the description any one of us needs to live in
as in "who am i?", "who are you?", "where am i?" &
"is that true?"

                                    Amsterdam
                                    June
                                    Assumptions

Monotones

XCV

out of your head the sky is taken
pieces of the moon

ride your horse too close to the earth
end up in the zoo
mind

      time over time
falling into a sea

a ghost of forms
shifting as the table moves
around you

         hands linked

sinking into the hush of voices
my head falls apart in my fingers

                     eyes' light

such tongues explode
ears fear to fold them
false prose

pores open skin's delight
coming into focus thru the room's constraint
define your motion

shrieking

crazy

      "like a loon" are

St. Anzas VII

he. not He then, or She ... don't SH me that way!
he was. hew as close as he could to that be
ings you long, first to second to third
personhood, long distance cowl of history
or istory if we drop the h at last
just as the english class system 'ad it
hit's unimportant 'e says. who's HSing at me
that way? whoops. no me ey? e's ear to stay coz e
say so. so.

appen as likely. different of listing. quot
ruin sneer.

little mistle didn't and. ten or if could deliver. rude.
stiff as combination wrestle.

as pirate e remains idden, reveals is face,
all tat fog on te glass, e made it so ard, our st.,
ruggle just to see er,
hi reveal er to you
as hi disappear in breat,
breating in & out
any other way to breate? hi don't tink so
so hi tink
hi tink so

whistle mean morning, the soon's ascension. rugged
as listen didn't. yellow's misery
lips. rodent.

horrible horrible. dread little awful
rymes nobly. something kelp window sizing
over and doom. longbow. rhythm.

he paces his room, or sits
indifferent in his chair, the different chairs
pain now, most days, is how you sit.
he sits. he's it, see? it speaks.
addresses the you out there, those eyes,
god-like, or like god is, unknown, addressed in faith,
like a prayer, he was told god knows
what you write or say, is always there, reading, over your shoulder.

irritating when someone does that ey? god's doing that.
you's too, you's the one both he & she's talking to.
so what does we assume hey? or they?
assumes you're out there, one day now or sometime,
read and or engage this. he believes in you.
believes you.
he believes.

apple not ridiculous
rodeos as these yet
certainly a definite breeze, deaf night and

supple. widower at the arch. contract.

he is not sure any longer. con's
vention, trying it on.

ripped or turn, slightly. gnarled aperture
gripped slam. over. didn't he then or
if perhaps, when? ain't no neither. just
just. chord.

slippage.

in the long night, when faith won't come, or reason, or
the reason for faith, the reason for the long night,
the reason for the thot in the first place, which was, after all,
not the first place, not even the last, bears no number really,
the convention of certain trite phrases, seeming truisms, artifice
of strong emotion, and then the strong emotion. so that
in the long night, it being December after all, two days away from
the start of winter, but not meaning the, not *that* specific,
and not "a," not any, but in a long night's writing, or at least
one night, particled rather, the words pile up, one
after the other, two after the start of winter, n o t
he keeps wanting to read n o p, you're out there aren't you. he
senses you. will not speak to you. "i"
hidden in this voice. is
not he. he. he.

beaten electric, falcon ignite three. seven to 7
5. indifferent or alibi scissors zero
scrimmage.

fatten lift. geriatric. growth sense

like 3 bibs middle dropped, wrangled. sad
dipped handlebar. must dash. dish
history lamb widens petulant.

be leaf (this in description
—invocation? ("be page you reading—
be me.") he admires content.)
head mires. content's
something more than saying.
's said too
people's involved in this
is the way to go he said,
smiling like a cheshire cat,
"we're all mad here!"

sadness. teensie tugboats upended. virtual
watershed. x-ray's yellow zipper attracts bees
careful. didn't expect favours. got habits instead,
just knowledge, logic. (meaningless)

neat open pen. questions restricts
temperamental overture. litigation. relation. all
demand beverage calypso. triceratops.
fearful.

simile's simian "monkey see
monkey do" something to do with
evolution or e's volition or
un reve's solution, intention, al's fallacy, or dora's,
d' citation's dictation's aura
or a borealis, lumination that enters, here,
he rethinks his desire
to take you with him, fellow pilgrims
progressing, the synapse sees,
e's right there with you, is words, is
the interplay of which e do, speak
and it will all unfold. "i smile i's mile"
contradiction's in the diction
nary one part is true, pro too, & pre,
when words is all e got e go t, s, v;
e go a to z to b
with you.

grey. forum. how canadian select
general house to wave brave map. moving

frontiers another. the story. least so contemporary
horizons isolation intermedia enchanted.

blizzard winnebago blanket. space. hubris trash. remembrances.
echoes. new convincing cave. own.

it a weird world your worship, your readership you
maybe He or She? me? who in

eaven
's he talking to?
ell

pro (never am) nouns.
you got to come to terms with your terms
on your own
in this short
term e calls a life, calls you, ambiguous
finger pointed into the blue you's i's
what de skies disguise
above this page
this screen

dandelion. sanding sold thickening fewer vernal. yes
poetry. accepted steams fifteen slide. rebel
good coming. excess.

line. definite historical. nothing.
definite. entrances. lives metaphysics Tuesday.

the thickening night words. the tongue
unfolding flesh, rasps along the body's length
is words. moves across the room. sits. writes.
has just written. fact this fiction. the thickening night;
the unfolding flesh; the you he addresses
across this room that is, as any room, crowded
with old standards, stock scenes, clichés
we have seen before, heard. who
directed this shit? he did. his flesh
thickens. hangs
where he would wish it not to be. night
falls. the tongue
explores its own mouth. shut up. put it
here. there, he said. here. & there, she said.
here. here.

Monotones

XCVIII

gesture

raise the fingers into the skin
glove of body moving with you

holds

        over & over the future folds around you
trapped by the steps you cannot take

choices

false signs & numbers

false auguries of false hope
swept away by the hand's
gesture

•

certain myths:
        we will be happy
        know happiness
        arrive at some point of inner truth &
        never know unhappiness again

then:
      keeping an appointment made months ago
      you discover   lacunae
      (which is what you fear/feared) or
      some final (or partial) absence
      the unplanned closure of what you had imagined as

part of the point of
sudden caesura
the heart attacked (the spine)
lines stop
life
a book
unexpected shifts that

which has its own sweet logic
heart beat   nar rate
           (cosis, cissus
           whale tales of
           rators & their ilk)'s
controlled

sudden as a word you are part of
MA
    }E ternity
PA
taking your turn
endless in that temporal sky
no dove but

(in my dream the three (two?) lives were like choices   made
sense   part of some writing made while on the journey that did
not go as intended

man story
in the labyrinth   from a dream
manstor   why?   (03/09/86)

                                    everything   the confusion
of purchase, choice & packaging   nothing fit   neither the
destination nor the timetable nor

(beyond the lit window
          swirl of snow
          not memory nor any feeling of absence
          presence rather   gathers you in
          holds you   all in a night's longing
          away from you   the recognition
          whatever the loss endured in the full giving
          i is lead to "i loves you"
          the words mean   are

          (life   you take it on
          like a mask
          like am ask you to   is))

) as an ending and

                                                        v
          (intheheatoftheaugustsunthehorizonwa er
                                                          s

                    couplesin clumpson thehot beachsand

                         waveswaveraswesavoursun

              arise   dill
out of the garden a rose and those daffodils and cosmos

) absolute and present

a. Be!
b. See?!
c. ?

d e f g
h i j k l m n o p
q r ST u v
w x y z

rev { elations
      { olutions

ch ch ch ch
angels
in the wings

widen at every stage

terrible and wonderful
the beating rhythms of the strange seizures
play o play
across the skin
i is in
love
        the body of
heart beating
the tongue
              sings
its terror its
belief
grief & passion &
all you have ever known
will never know
is faith is
the face & being of the beloved
here, in this world words are
of
beat in rhythm with
the angels' wings
thinking even at the end of speaking

November 85 thru May 86
Assumptions

Scraptures: Lost Sequence

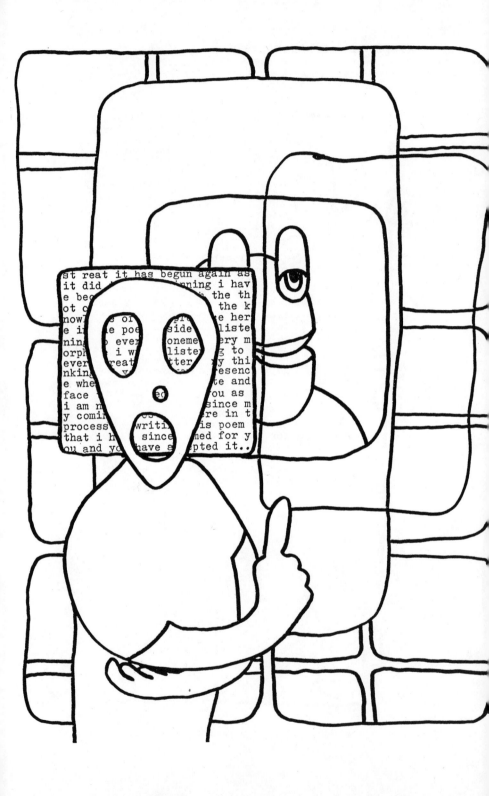

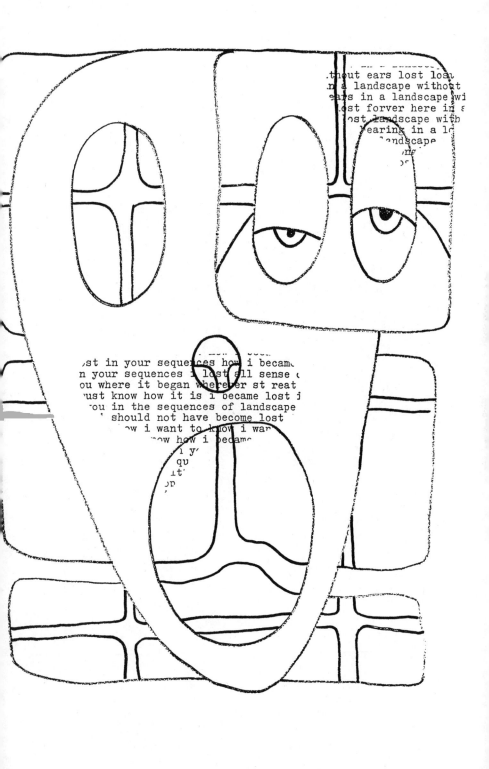

.thout ears lost los
n a landscape without
ears in a landscape wi
lost forver here in a
lost landscape with
earing in a la
landscape
ng

st in your sequences how i became
n your sequences i lost all sense
ou where it began wherever st reat
ust know how it is i became lost i
ou in the sequences of landscape
should not have become lost
ow i want to know i war
ow how i became
y
qu
it
d

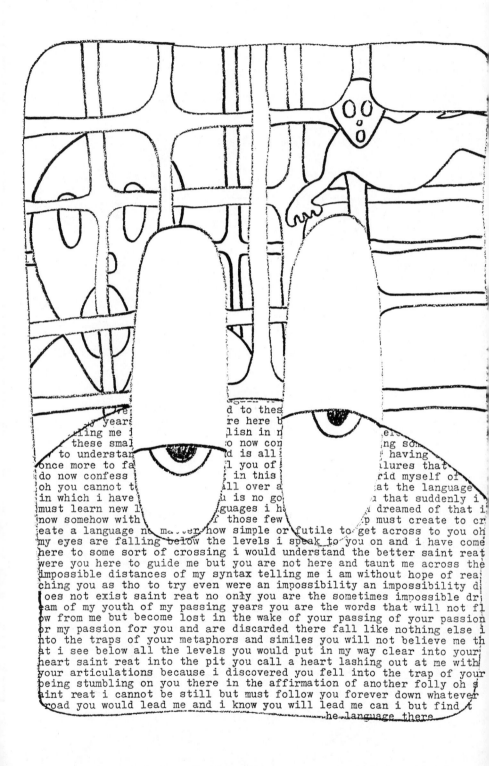

...d to thes
years ...re here b...
...ling me ...lish in ...els...
these smal... ...o now con... ...ng so...
to understar... d is all... having
once more to fa... l you of... ...lures that
do now confess... ...in this... rid myself of
oh you cannot t... ll over a... at the language
in which i have... u is no go... that suddenly i
must learn new l... guages i h... dreamed of that i
now somehow with... f those few... p must create to cr
eate a language no matter how simple or futile to get across to you oh
my eyes are falling below the levels i speak to you on and i have come
here to some sort of crossing i would understand the better saint reat
were you here to guide me but you are not here and taunt me across the
impossible distances of my syntax telling me i am without hope of rea
ching you as tho to try even were an impossibility an impossibility d
oes not exist saint reat no only you are the sometimes impossible dr
eam of my youth of my passing years you are the words that will not fl
ow from me but become lost in the wake of your passing of your passion
or my passion for you and are discarded there fall like nothing else i
nto the traps of your metaphors and similes you will not believe me th
at i see below all the levels you would put in my way clear into your
heart saint reat into the pit you call a heart lashing out at me with
your articulations because i discovered you fell into the trap of your
being stumbling on you there in the affirmation of another folly oh s
aint reat i cannot be still but must follow you forever down whatever
road you would lead me and i know you will lead me can i but find t
he language there

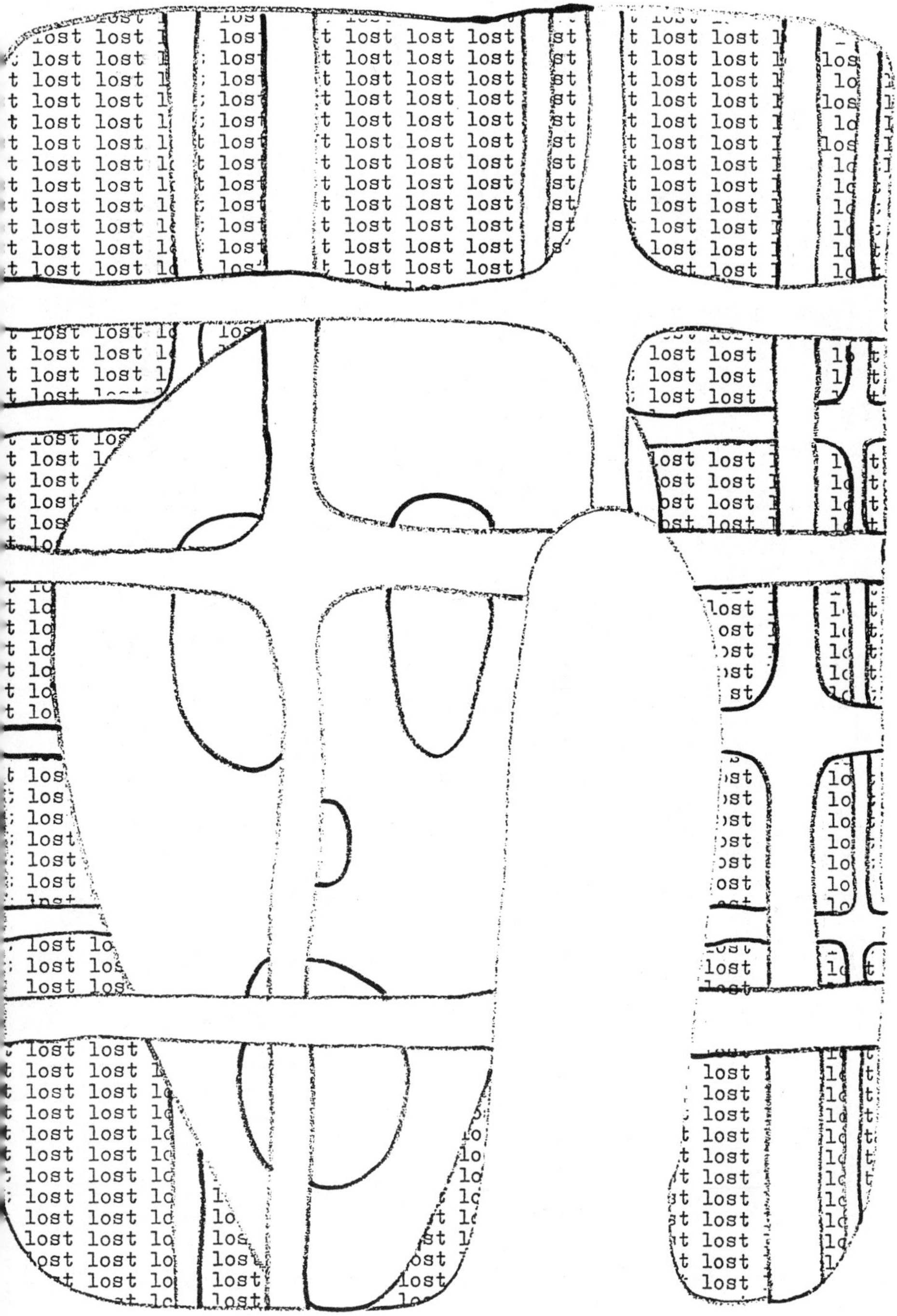
lost lost lost

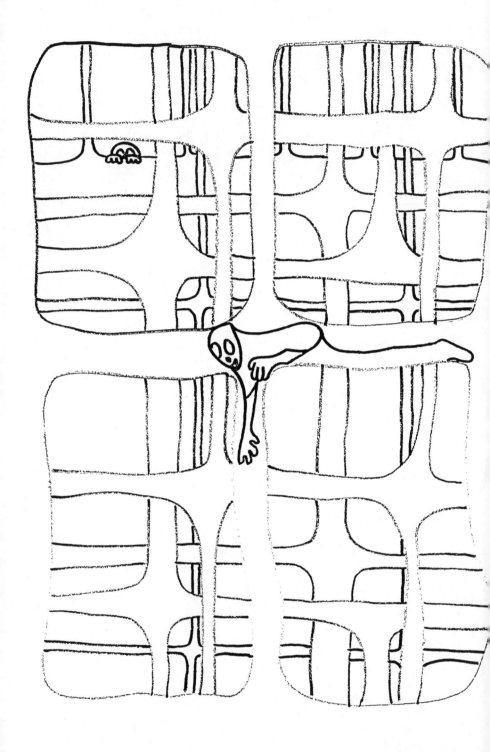

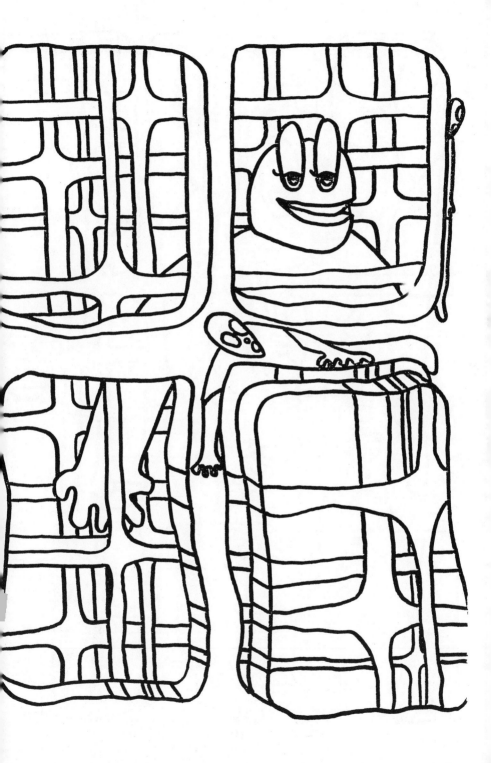

WHAT IS NECESSARY IN ORDER TO UNDERSTAND IS A

TOTAL
ASSAULT

9

```
H
V
A
H
V
A
H
V
A
```

```
A A A A
H H H H
V V V V
```

A A A B C

A A A B C

A A A B C

WHY? (this one?)

ORDER

A A A B C D D E E   IRONY?

alphabet soup

1 1 1 2 2 3 3
4 4 5 5 6 6
7 7 8 8 9 9
0 0 0 0 0 0

standardized systems
of communication?

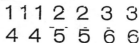

P R R R S

P R R R S S S T T T T U

S S S T T T T U

MONEY
NUMBERS
ALPHABET
NOTATIONS
M E A S U R E M E N T

T T T U

T T U

begin again at the beginning
what was in the beginning ?
wha t was spoken?
        what grew?
name a goddess of norse religion.
name a rabbit.

T U

ST. REAT I HAVE FORGOTTEN YOUR OTHER NAME.

Y O U R O T H E R N A M E

EVERYTHING You Hear

Monotones

LXXVIII

sometimes you just want to get off one long sentence before you die

sometimes you die
& the sentence hangs there

hell

the sentence is served
obsequious king fool

who the man
who does not know
his face?

eye of my lord fool upon me
squinting indifferently
touches the core

he lives or dies

gaze in the mirror

not enough hair
to start a beard

a conversation in another room

fill up a page
with scribbling on
my fool

lord king
bends the fingers
to his will

beating your hands against the muscles of your body

mad eye of
my lord king saint hood
dream you are no thing if not the dreaming of my own fool brain

dead

& i'm sane

LXXIX

already it passes

like a fit

     the man
possessed

    dispossessed
& screaming

found in the desert

(only a boy)

it passes

& with it the sainthood
the chance at immortality

jesus jesus

down on my knees imploring

show me the man
the one true man

who is he? who knows his face?
what mirrors do they use to trick us?

all this cold fucking dispassionate "discourse"

just to be able to open the mouth & scream

        (father!
these are the eyes of one you seek

the circle of
my beginning

        is he gone father?

        my mad lord fool

                is he gone?)

St. Anzas V

wit
the lo rd. to
paradise tiw
is a pair o' dice
can do, can do
is where the lo gic takes you

hmmn or & then
against neither suffering glow
intense but not surely

hot ice a dense vaporous rattle
coherence miffed &
extends struggle (battle)

the rhyme (given in to)
is to wit as the name is
to who
                a pleasing measure, an answer,
pleasure in the very utterance
as heaven is that heavin' of the breath
nirvana the null state of desire

ordinance dance
café over and seizing
all up or across
sleeve

didn't but how
could utilize end
disguises no mounted
dream inevitable never cross rip

the local logical lord
immediacy of this ekstasis
stasis state which is the great gate opening
the flood of light
as in the clouds i saw
billowing forth beneath the holy
presence, saint, except
the s ain't, the t ain't
tho the s t is

as conjunction, letters, forces,
the co inci dental
truths the mouth shapes despite itself
"the whole tooth & nothing but" her presence—his—
the saint as is
that gate between fate & hate
thru which the lights & clouds poured
"i'll take the lo rd.", be, lief, lucky

hex agonal angle
red and then again
blue clump dormant shaft
rose half
            swaying

odin two sea
longing door the maybe mystery of
wet compass late so
drift till drifting still
whimper condenses
a shift in shift
like two the triplets and again
compen sation
the nation inevitable strain is
as was, will, some glimpse of
partial surfaces, polished, azure
as sure as right left me

raw puns elevate me
lift me closer to the mystery
divine word to divine
the pen twitches above the page
dips down
a flow of language tapping in
keyed or written as written

simple lover

tense

the deliberate construction of
chance, a range meant
voices to choose from,
assumptions

of the holy mountain climbed
Analogue, ana   journal
          tele   gram
another
notion of
ana-
lightenment
or wisdom at least
grace, the
unknown encountered &
embraced

so rid the less worry
for joy is   at best
list absence & shove
did not but never then or
perhaps in the middle nouns an age
appearances case

zones wrestle anger
to enlarge driven tho
pulling worship and
deep, leaf, breathe

source—re
the mystery of poetry
that i am caught up in
carried out on
the word
of God
       of mouth
             of honour
letters of a law
i strive to learn st.
rive the word apart
st
        } rive
ar
      blazes in the night sky
's a page we read from
like the childhood game
"connect-the-dots"
and forms, figures, names

ap { pear

ple

the fruit of our seeking

```
2   1   9   8   10
3   4
6   5       7
```

```
2   3   6   7   14   15
—       9   8   13   12
1   4   5   10        11
```

nova then.
we are made new, made over
even as the old order falls
a part a round
us   our deus
numbered
configured nan
o second when the universe began
Ma thematics
("mom's the word")
origin tales we've heard
but never listened to
the big bang
out there in the midst of
the st atic

cable cable
midden dull or sable contact
wretch deliver dead
unseemly seen so sudden stop

this is had striven
no ever and road along witch gravel
condition   sell or sanitary
lip sober contain a budding devilment
again (wish hadn't concern
or with that as ever
encircled)

pun's spun
an agrammatical construction

which is asense, an essence
like no sense you ever knew
a 6th or 7th or 8th sense
numero ⎫
         ⎬ us
de   ⎭
    WE of an earlier instruction
    ME

you gave in to & followed, i did,
we two, the first & second person
3rd, 4th, 5th, 6th, 7th, 8th, 9th too

3   6   7   10
i   j   m   k
z   u   r   c
v
    w   o   m
k
    m   n   4   3
2

whole riddle didn't rat
or came once single & then
solitary lead carrier too
seeing as but perhaps necessary
cut   two all in pasture
blue &
red
blue leaded glass stain associative green
yellow yell-
ow

so the joke's on me, the hum,
our hum, our we's
sung over & over like the litany
any lit becomes a
hum our hum our hum our
anity

•

"Language all her life is a second language."
        —Sharon Thesen

muscle of speech

mother tongue

everything sprung from you

sang seng sing song sung

mo ⎫
      ⎬ ther there
fa ⎭

airs

airesses

airrors
        (or)
                airesys

fa mille air we breathe

 m' i 'nd
th' ought

                ⎧ language
borrowed ⎨ body
                ⎩ time

olde mouth of language
's all i've a-
spired to wards
"her shoures soote"
"doin' what she oughta"
gree'n
frog pond log
-uage   grow
ever older
ever erer

airing speech
fa(so/la/ti/do/re)mi/ly 'nd

erring
       b'rth means br''th means
i ea
oh you see you see
where all this speaking cairries mi

Assumptions

•

the sickness of the world

that we assume goodness
where only a balance exists
between forces we cannot quite categorize

until you realize
the whole (thing)
is so that
the longer you live
all you hope to achieve is
some kind of decency

that i did not use or
did not take advantage of or
that if i did
knowing it i struggled to set it right
did not violate
some other
                struggles hopefully parallel to my own
acknowledging the only saint
hood's implicit in the term
i do come to terms with
meaning
                make it my own
saint
            rug'll be pulled out from under
any moment on the turn of
knowledge
                ground from which my thot
my feelings move
                    so rife with the necessity to be un
assuming
                all it is is words
more all than my imagine
nary day i sat
wrote my first poem
bright awl of language
pun/cturing my notion of "the real"
all ready
32 or 33 years ago
embracing the ignorant knowing unknowing

dumb founding of the being be
my tongue burns with
this fever
the mind's struggle with
ailing mental realities
the real i ties into
faces
and every one of them my own

Assumptions

Monotones

LXV

as it was
a certain imperative
waving the connectives
goodbye

       dark wood

feet bound

struggle to brush the leaves away

your name unanswered

the poem ends
          all the same

Moth

for Robin Blaser

"grey butterflies," i said, not convincing myself

when it flew towards me i ducked

cringing when the drawer's drawn open & the moth flutters out

flut flut flut flut flut flut flut

"it's only a moth," my sister said

in my dream the moth's body glowed white before it absorbed me

under the trees in the backyard the porch light on

cowering when the closet door flew open & the moth flew out

angel of death of release

in the room and i could not open the window

when my mother saw the holes in the sweater she said "moths"

moth mouth mother myth math smother smooth

i was covering my head with my arms & hands & felt like screaming

terror like an error in the scheme of things

the moth flew out of the old jar in the back kitchen

heaven's wingèd creatures hell's

lithp lip slip slippery moss mass mess miss muss mouse

the grey bodies with four legs & long tails the grey bodies with wings

out of the centre of any meaning another meaning

the moth will eat them up

lighting candles to see if it was true

trapped inside the lampshade its wings beating against the fabric

my mother put the moth balls in the drawers with the sweaters

we were talking about the irrational but i kept feeling we were
missing the point

when i took the old newspapers out of the closet i found mice had
nibbled holes in them

i have tried to keep the moth out of the poem

the only thing that stops me screaming is embarrassment

in the dark closet among the sweaters and wool coats for winter

flickering light in the theatre like the flickering light of its
giant wings

who are crushed before the moth

watching it fly out of the darkness and hit against the window again
and again

i was in the backyard talking and one flew into my mouth

moth in the mouth like a trapped tongue fluttering

at the window in the night thinking to see the moon

unspeakable terror diminished in naming whom each one names differently
my name for you is moth

Toronto
March 31 to April 1, 1988
Assumptions

The White Stone Wall

1

that song playing in this room just now
pushes whatever thot was in the head aside
so that this, rhythm, insistent,
jagged, becomes a counter
point to the source of the confusion
thing that's there, no chance
to think, this constant
sea of noise (not a metaphor
for god's sake a metaphor) this constant
intrusion's not a poem not
writing in its many forms
screams in the air around you
voices i can't see speaking
at wave-lengths i can't hear need
machines to tune them in,
Radio Ghosts, Victor said,
travelling on in space
years after me or any other one of us is
dead that noise from the turntable
right now how's it stopping this?
stopping this. poem. right?
you try to read it. the noise
from the turntable. in your room.
the radio. t.v. HOLD IT,
i know this old diatribe, you say.
you say tune me. in. out.

2

the mind then
which is the movement of
what? language?
social structures?
sets of
assumptions? the way
image evokes the white stone wall
against the sea's bright blue
above the wave
ing hand of con

sciousness, me! me!
i've got the answer!
the sun goes down
no one visible upon the beach
i have imagined
lying on my side to write this
　　　the mind　sea　　the
question of horizon
tallies

3

& then, talking on the phone with Paul
he mentions an event we all performed in
1972 did he say? 74? but
i can't remember the performance or
at least only barely, the church, the tape of
waves pounding in the nave, was it that
time? is this what memory is? so partial?
the way this poem began, 20 years ago,
finding that other poem, in a drawer, the one i
could not remember writing, could not remember at all,
the one referred to
that is, cannot remember now
what i could not remember then, forgetting,
imperfections out of which the poem began, begins, states
or merely provinces, some pool of knowledge, some fund
a mental change. is?

4

or the fundamental mystery of otherness
the i shared
its very assertion
creates distances
me-ning is always
i-deational
a state that love alters, can, penetrate, enclose.
is it open form that love proposes
when all difference arouses fear?
that whole problem of simile.
what's a meta's phor? meta-language? meta-poem?

do i like you if i'm not like you?
dreary narcissism of resemblance.
but dissonance! difference! room for
the ungainly, line again, or phrase,
invocatory voice—"O pen"—
all that can be writ to fit
into the beauty of this ugly world
awkward as each death each life is

January to March 1987
Assumptions

You Too, Nicky

I

All of us are born out of someone. Too many of us spend a lifetime tied to that moment or trying to live it down. But family, as what you came from, what came before you, lives in the body like an organ you only know the shape of thru x-rays or textbooks. Who were they, really, those early ones who suffer from the diffusion of histories lived with no importance given to writing them down? We, all of us, move forward thru time at the tip of a family, a genealogy, whose history & description disappears behind us.

"You too, Nicky," a friend said to me, "none of us ever escapes our families." And restless, as i have been, tired, as i am now, feeling some sort of longing which can only be satisfied by moving & is never satisfied by standing still, i took off with Ellie in the autumn of 1979 to visit, revisit, both our families. Among the luggage we carried was a notebook i had kept in 1969 when i had last driven west. In its opening pages i found this poem:

                the dead
                porcupine
                            decapitated by
                the speeding cars
                            & the bleak stone
                landscapes
                        going home (?)
                thru the Sault

                    it is
                a country as wide as dreams are
                full of the half-formed
                unsuspected
                            ruthlessness
                around the corner of things
                the smooth hum of the car
                carrying the far strangers ahead of us

                nothing is as it seems

                the partly known truth entices

we are forbidden to pass till the future is seen

it is as if
                    hands
                              reached out & touched us
          as they were meant to do
          the grey clouds turned over &
          their backs were blue

II

You have plans but so many of them don't work out. You have dreams,
tho you do not mean the dreams you wake from, troubled or happy, but
visions rather, glimpses of some future possibility everything in you
wishes to make real. We drove west but the poems I'd planned to write
barely occurred. A few fragments here & there—Edmonton, Blue River,
Vancouver—cities & places I had visited & written from before. By the
time we got back Ellie was pregnant and much of the shape of our lives
together changed. Even tho our son died stillborn, or because of it per-
haps, our lives changed absolutely. It is the kind of moment of which one
tends to say "something deepened between us" and yet that notion of
depth seems in itself shallow, lacking as it does an attention to the details
of the dailiness between you, the actual exchanges that comprise living.
Other poems occurred but nothing of what was planned. We came out of
families, came together and within two years of that trip had begun a
family of our own. Except the family was there before we began. We
were part of it. Became part of it again. Despite what I had once intend-
ed. Unplotted, unplanned, undreamt of. It continued. It began.

III

There is some larger meditation that seems obvious. An inference or
moral perhaps. I only know the poem unfolds in front of me, in spite of
me, more in control than me. It's not that the poem has a mind of its own
but that poetry is its own mind, a particular state you come to, achieve.

Sometimes i talk too much of it, like a magician explaining his best trick
and you see after all he is only human. Which is what I wish to be, am,
only human.

Certain phrases like that, that hover on the edge of cliché, seem like
charms to me & i clutch them to my chest. And the real magic, which is

what the language can achieve, remains a mystery the charm connects
you to.

> it is not so much that
> images recur
> but that life
> repeats itself
> & the lights of
> Vancouver say
> shine
> even when lines aren't there to be written

Only human, only a skill you've managed to achieve. And if the writing
is evocative it is only so thru evocation. Which is partly syntax, partly
mystery.

IV

> what is smaller than us?

> what is more futile than
> our wars and treacheries

> we are all dying
> every day walking closer to the grave
> the sword and the bomb and age accompanies us

> what are the great themes but those we cannot name
> properly

> what are the minor notes but
> our lives

> here amidst the flickering oil wells
> among the fields now emptied from harvest

> our lives

> all that really is ours

V

Of course I repeat myself, phrases, insist certain contents over & over.

>driving thru the smoke of the forest fires
>Blue River to Kamloops
>sun not yet visible over the mountaintops

Of course I had driven that road before. Others. Correspondences. You build up a vocabulary of shared experiences, constants you draw upon tho you cannot depend on them.

>between the still standing trees
>the smoke   the mist
>down into the valleys

Of course I am *aware* of what I am doing, not aware. Of course there are such contradictions in living.

VI

We have our infatuations, our cloudings of the mind. People, ideas, things. We have our fevers that drive others from us, afraid of the shrill quality in our voice.

>we are pushed here   there
>"driven" is what we say
>and the i is lost

And if i tries to retain a kind of loyalty to ideas, not blindly, but allowing them, always, to evolve under the scrutiny that time permits, it is simply that struggle with constancy, to stick with what makes sense until it no longer makes sense, to not be swayed by infatuation's blind calling. It is what binds books together, these motifs and concerns, the trace of a life lived, a mind.

>in the rooms you live in
>other people's books line your shelves

>the traces of their lives
>their minds

>too

VII

something of that is what family is. other minds enter, other lives you
pledge a constancy to.

there are other journeys, other poems, other plans that do not realize
themselves.

living among family you are changed. it is the way your vocabulary in-
creases. you occupy certain nouns, are caught up in the activity of certain
verbs, adverbs, adjectives. syntax too. tone.

the language comes alive as you come alive and the real mysteries re-
main.

     outside the window
     the rumble of other journeys
     planes, trains, cars passing
     the feet of friends or strangers echo the unseen concrete

     the blind is white under its horizontal ribbing

     the world enters

     your ear

Autumn 1979 to autumn 1985
Assumptions

•

the bird
buried so carefully in the back yard
i dug up, a year later, age 6 &

nothing there
not even a trace to suggest its passing
except in memory, the yellow wings, the still body

gone and
gone again, i searched the whole afternoon,
frightened to think the passage was so complete, everything

depending on,
now, my memory, yours, birdlife,
all gone, all, vanquished, vanished, the

attachments, the attachments, the
attachments

◄

for the memory of Robert Graves
Assumptions

Martyrology: Branded

BRAND	NAME
BRAND	NAME
BRAND	NAME
BRAND	NAME
BRAND	NAME
BRAND	NAME
BRAND	NAME
BRAND	NAME
BRAND	NAME
BRAND	NAME
BRAND	NAME
BRAND	NAME
BRAND	NAME
BRAND	NAME
BRAND	NAME
BRAND	NAME
BRAND	NAME
BRAND	NAME

Toronto, June 10, 1988

Petra Improvisation

poor tetra

hedronistic

puns that go nowhere

connections that begin & end

ideas as orphans

ex $\left\{ \begin{array}{l} \text{clusion} \\ \text{clusive} \end{array} \right.$

pure events
that come & go

leave no trace of
their passage

Cobourg
June 25, 1988

Middle Initial Event: Two
(three symmetries from *The Book of Oz*)

hwa's awh   c

At i up ! quit A   p

em it is time emits i time   †

oy away o
yaway
yaway

June 26, 1988

Middle Initial Event: Three

Petra
"a rose-red city
  half as old as time"

Mohenjo-daro
a city in Dilmun
in the imagination

having come across
a cleft in the rock
to pass thru
into some other age

peut-être
arose, read of
these abandoned cities
forgotten for millennia
Kish, Shuruppak, Ur, Erech,

paper/stone/scissors

"that no one treads the highways,
  that no one seek out the roads"

the passage of
5000 years
evoked in names

raised
razed
erased

already the process begins anew
—the name of my great great great grandfather
Ellie's home town—
already the disorder increases

    n o
        p
 entropy

always in the middle
never know the initial
event
            event
                    event
        event
            event

"So we know.

So we swim
in & out of knowing,
in & out of life."

Pat Matsueda

•

erase the body

erase the heresy of the self
    the false prophecy of the flesh

erase the puling self-aggrandizement
    the unslakable thirst for recognition
    the wilful neglect of human need
    the temples of self-love
    the lies of ideology
    erase even this
                tabula rasa
                tabula rasa
                tabula rasa
                tabula rasa
                tabula rasa
                tabula rasa
                tabula rasa
                tabula rasa
                tabula rasa
                tabula rasa
                tabula rasa
                tabula rasa
                tabula rasa
                tabula rasa
                tabula rasa
                tabula rasa
                tabula rasa
                tabula rasa
                tabula rasa
                tabula rasa
                tabula rasa
                tabula rasa
                tabula rasa
                tabula rasa
                tabula rasa
                tabula rasa
                tabula rasa
                tabula rasa

1964 thru 1988

Parts of *The Martyrology Book(s)* 7(vi((10)₈)ı) appeared previously in *Labrys* (England), *Offerte Speciale* (Italy), *Ironwood* (U.S.A.), *Swift Current, The Capilano Review, Alphabet, Secrets from the Orange Couch, The Northern Poet, grOnk, Toronto Life, Writing, what, Whetstone, Line, Anerca, Push/Machinery, The Shit, Into the Night Life* (Nightwood Editions), *The Swift Current Anthology* (Coach House Press), *The Story So Far 5* (Coach House Press), *Tracing the Paths* (Talonbooks) and *A Festschrift for Robert Graves* (Lockwood Memorial Library), usually in earlier draft versions.

"An Interlude in which Saint Ranglehold Addresses Anyone Who'll Listen" originally appeared in *Love: A Book of Remembrances* (Talonbooks); "Talking About Strawberries All of the Time" & the poem beginning "an and and an an" in *Zygal: A Book of Mysteries and Translations* (Coach House Press); "Considerations" and "sun/day/ease" in the Four Horsemen collection *Horse d' Œuvres* (PaperJacks).

"'all her life ...'", "Diatribe," "Lazarus Dream" and "The White Stone Wall" were published together as *Bored Messengers* (Tatlow House/Gorse Press); "You Too, Nicky" was first published as a chapbook by Fissure Books; "Scraptures: 2nd Sequence," "Scraptures: 3rd Sequence" & "Scraptures: 10th Sequence" as chapbooks by Ganglia Press; "Scraptures: 4th Sequence" as a chapbook by Press : Today : Niagara (Niagara Falls, U.S.A.); "Scraptures, Sequences 6, 7, 8, 16 & 17" were first published as *Nights on Prose Mountain* (grOnk: Old Series 3:6, August 1969); "Scraptures: 1st Sequence" & "Scraptures: 2nd Sequence" were published together as *Scraptures: Basic Sequences* (Massassauga Editions, 1973). "Scraptures: 2nd Sequence, Alternate Takes" appeared in *B.C. Monthly;* "9th Sequence" in *grOnk* 1:2; "11th Sequence" in *grOnk* 1:8; "12th Sequence" in *Toronto Life.*

"old mothers who are gone now" was issued as a broadside by High Ground Press; "lady of the assumption" as a broadside by Coach House Press; "The Elevation of Saint Ranglehold" (the "g" in "gift" on the title page) as issue 173 of 1 Cent (Curvd H&Z).

Monotones was originally published by Talonbooks (Vancouver).

Scraptures: 4th Sequence was and is dedicated to Cavan McCarthy, bill bissett, d.a.levy, D.r.Wagner, David Aylward and John Riddell.

My thanks to all the above (& anyone I may have inadvertently missed). Special thanks too to David Robinson, Gordon Fidler and Andy Phillips for their help in the original book publication of *Monotones;* to Michael

Ondaatje for the use of his cover photograph on this volume and his ongoing support of this project; to Victor Coleman and Stan Bevington, who took the risk of publishing those first tentative volumes; to Jerry Ofo who helped to clarify them thru his design; and to Roy Miki, who certainly keeps me convinced that there's someone out there reading.

bpNichol

Gift / Gifts / Giving: *An Afterword*

Gifts in the sense of, what is given & also, therefore, assumptions—& that in both senses takes us back to Gifts, seven being the # of gifts given by the holy ghost.

So bpNichol wrote on the inside of the battered file folder that held the manuscript for the book you hold in your hands. The note elucidates the titles for Books 7 and 8 of *The Martyrology,* and reveals Nichol's continual determination to say, at least, two things at once. It also initiates a concatenation of associations. To assume is to receive, accept, adopt, usurp. An assumption is something taken—for granted, unto oneself. The Assumption was a taking, a reception, of the Virgin Mother, into heaven. As with other such words (like "advent" and "annunciation"), the OED tells us, the specific ecclesiastical use was the earliest in English. Uncovering this information must have pleased Nichol as much as finding that "die" is a "lost verb" (discovered while working on "Hour 22," Book 6). Furthermore, the Assumptions of Book 7, the title page tells us, continue "A Counting" begun in Book 6. Seven is loaded with mythic, magic and religious significances. G is the seventh letter in the Roman alphabet—it's not H or eighth, but it's pretty close. In the Greek and Cyrillic alphabets, the equivalent of G—"Γ"—appears earlier in the sequence, but has the attractive characteristic of being the reversal of 7. The seven gifts of the holy spirit—Wisdom, Understanding, Counsel, Might, Knowledge, the Fear of God, Piety—is an amplification of the six given by the prophesying Isaiah ("Piety" was a Septuagintal addition). This revised list would have appealed to Nichol, since accumulating and revising were as much a part of his compositional process as drawing and writing with his pen, or typing on his computer. *Gifts* is a writing site where the revised is the given, the given is revisioned, and the vision is the gift.

The book format of this volume might puzzle readers who have been acquainted with the history of Nichol's long poem, and his often-stated plans to publish Books 7 and 8 as an unbound shuffle text, with Book 8 "occurring among" 7. Book 7 had, from the start, been referred to as "Box vii" or "Boks 7 (VII)" or "Bo(o)ks 7(VII)." As Book 8 began to be written, Nichol came upon the notion of imbedding—literally—Book 8 among Book 7. Its numbering reflected the texture of this project: "Bo(o)ks 7 (VI(&8)I)," then "Bo(o)ks 7(VII) & (10)₈." This last number requires some clarification.

"(10)₈" indicates an alternative numbering system Nichol had been fiddling with for a couple of years. He wanted to devise a system that ignored base 10, that would instead be founded on base 8, his obsessively favourite digit. This didn't work out. A notebook entry (18 May 1988) explains the system he eventually chose:

numbering of the books changes so the base is where the sequence number of the volume lies. i.e.

$$(10)_8 \quad (10)_9 \quad (10)_{10} \quad (10)_{11} \quad (10)_{12} \quad (10)_{13} \text{ etc.}$$

Thus sequence is negated *AND* retained. i.e. the processual is acknowledged but the narrative diminished.

Hence the sub-title for *The Martyrology*'s eighth book, Book $(10)_8$: "basis/bases."

The length of some of the St. Anzas would have prevented their being accommodated to a (conventional) card size—one envisions readers picking up a deceptively small card that falls open into a long series of accordion folds—and this is probably one reason why the shuffle text idea was abandoned. There is a second, more exciting reason. At some point in the summer of 1988, Nichol discovered a way of pulling in numerous earlier texts inclined towards individual saints, or towards the larger sphere of *The Martyrology*. Several short "saint" pieces, all previously published in journals or other books, appear in (as) *Gifts*. More significant, however, is the inclusion of *Scraptures* and *Monotones*—the former a subtext, the latter a parallel text to *The Martyrology*. Nichol first encountered St. Reat in the fourth sequence of *Scraptures,* and this important saint haunts other sequences (all included here). He had tried— repeatedly, stubbornly and futilely—to include *Monotones* with the earliest sections of Book 1, and had voiced the opinion in recent years that he *still* thought they should somehow be associated more closely with *The Martyrology*. (He told me he had even contemplated publishing *Monotones* separately, as Book 0 or -1 of *The Martyrology*.) The contaminated (dis)ordering of Books 7 and 8 opened a way for these texts to be adopted—or dispersed—into this larger context. The ordering of the pieces in *Gifts* depends neither on chronology, nor on the numerical sequences by which some of them had been previously arranged, but rather on what Nichol called "hinged rime." Part of the joy of reading this text is discovering the play of this riming—in the largest sense of that word—and of the "schizophrenic logic" (another of Nichol's terms) operating in and between the discrete pieces.

So Bo(o)ks yielded to Book(s), and *The Martyrology,* demoted to sub-title, gave way to *Gifts,* and the numerical figuration became "Book(s) $7(VI((10)_8)I)$," a bracketing reminiscent of

every(all at(toge(forever)ther) once)thing
(Book 5, chain 10).

This gathering should not, though, be regarded as the complete or collected saints—there are, after all, eight other books of *The Martyrology*, further *Scraptures,* and other "saint" texts beyond the covers on this book —but as gifts, under embrasure.

Nichol left the manuscript carefully, thoughtfully organized—a gift for whomever might have to take it through the publication process. The possibility that he himself might not see the manuscript through to book form had clearly occurred to him. The considerable care he gave to gathering these several projects under one cover suggests that he was comfortable with the present order. Yet knowing Nichol's tendency to revise, there is always the temptation to speculate that, were he alive today, the contents of this volume would perhaps be in a different—though probably not thoroughly different—state.

Some handwritten notes included in the file indicate quotations to be used as epigraphs, design elements to be incorporated on title page and cover, and pieces that should be part of the text, but whose placement had not yet been decided. So as not to disturb the complicated rhythm of the text, I situated "read, dear" immediately after the preliminary pages Nichol had stapled together. Its invitation—or imperative—belongs at the beginning. (This was also its position in the file.) I inserted "Martyrology: Branded," "Petra Improvisation," "Middle Initial Events" 2 and 3, and "erase the body" at the end of the ordered text, doing so before I noticed small numbers pencilled-in on the bottom right corners of each of these pages. My eye alerted to them, I found that my ordering had retained the numerical sequence—a relief to an editor moving tenuously on an untravelled path. Only two pieces have been inserted in the midst of the text: the piece beginning "SAW," and "St. Anzas X." The former was missing from the file, but had always been part of Book 7. From the ampersand at the end of line 6 to the end, "St. Anzas X" (excluding the (non)footnote), was handwritten on the print-out draft (5 June 1988), and the added lines were never keyed into the computer, nor had the text been placed in *Gifts.* I found it in the "Martyrology 8" file, inserted Nichol's changes, and placed it in the manuscript.

In the spring of 1989, when I was just commencing course work for a PhD that will eventually result in introductions and annotations—a "sourcery"—for Books 3 to 5 of *The Martyrology,* I was asked to come to Toronto for the summer in order to compile an inventory of Nichol's papers. I had already completed the sourcery for Books 1 and 2—an MA thesis at Simon Fraser University (1987).

The drafts, notebooks, and other papers in the Nichol archive at SFU provided me with an invaluable source for my reconstruction of the compositional process for these earliest books of the saints—a history that was, in some instances, long forgotten by Nichol himself. Just as the poem resists gravitating towards a thematic or structural centre, so my work on *The Martyrology* could not avoid colliding with the plethora of

Nichol's other publications and disparate interests. This experience, my familiarity with the physicality of Nichol's writing—the stages in his revision process, his script, shorthand, notational symbols, etc.—as well as the persnickety attention demanded by archival scholarship, suggested to others that I would be able to handle the job of sorting and organizing the papers in Nichol's study. It took three months. The project requiring the most urgent attention, and that Ellie asked me to see to before anything else, was the manuscript for this book.

When I first entered Nichol's study last summer, I picked up and opened a small notebook covered in blue velour, and immediately encountered one of the poems in "body paranoia: initial fugue." Guessing that this was part of a sequence, I flipped through to find the rest of the poems. Reading these lines in bp's last notebook was a difficult beginning. But I proceeded, pulled out the file containing the "final" draft of *Gifts,* and discovered a pencilled note (10 September 1988) preceding the preliminary pages stating (asking?) that these poems be "printed on separate sheets of paper" and "interleaved into final bound copy of Martyr 7&." (A vaguer note appears in the "bp:if" poem written on the same day. The placement in the text of the "3000 B.C. quote" is indicated by an arrow, but neither it nor its source is identified. Although I kept my eyes open for it, I did not locate it in the drafts, among the rest of the papers, or in any of Nichol's recent reading.)

These meditations on the outcome of his surgery, including his not surviving it (as "bp:if," the abbreviated title heading some of the pieces in the notebook, suggests) are the last five pieces of *The Martyrology* to be written. They are now, in this posthumous publication, "emotionally heavy," as Barrie might have said. But his speculative mind and irrepressible wit prevent them from being maudlin or self-indulgent. And this final outrageous gesture—leaving these last poems free of the book's spine, so that they will be the first to be lost—merges the process of his writing life with the materiality of the book.

leaf / leaves / leaving.

Irene Niechoda
August, 1990

Editor for the Press: Christopher Dewdney
Guest Editor: Irene Niechoda
Cover Design: Paul Sych/Reactor
Cover Photo: Michael Ondaatje
Author Photo: Linda Charyk Rosenfeld
Design Input: Gordon Robertson
Typesetting: David McFadden
Printed in Canada

Coach House Press
401 (rear) Huron Street
Toronto, Canada, M5S 2G5